Association for Project Management
Ibis House, Regent Park
Summerleys Road, Princes Risborough
Buckinghamshire
HP27 9LE

British Library Cataloguing in Publication Data is available
ISBN 10: 1-903494-47-8
ISBN 13: 978-1-903494-47-9

Table of contents

Contents

Preface

The *Earned Value Management Handbook* is the culmination of the Association for Project Management's Planning, Monitoring and Control Specific Interest Group's (SIG) work to date.

It represents the effort of practitioners, academics and other stakeholders who have all given their time, knowledge and experience.

There is no finer testament to the idea that peer to peer conversation produces work of substance and value, while fostering a sense of collective purpose, achievement and service.

To all who have contributed, this book is for you and your communities.

This is only the end of the beginning. I am hopeful that this work will help you keep calm and carry on.

Good luck and let us know how you get on.

You can help by contributing to the next edition.

Steve Wake

Steve Wake
APM Planning, Monitoring and Control SIG Chairman

Foreword

In 2008, I was asked to write the foreword to the *Earned Value Management: APM Guidelines*. It provided the reader with a solid grounding in the 'why' and 'what' of earned value that needs to be done to ensure successful project implementation and delivery.

That publication did not include the detailed information on how to implement and use such a system. This handbook provides that missing link. APM's Planning, Monitoring and Control Specific Interest Group (SIG) has drawn upon a vast array of experience to create not just an EV handbook; it is also linked to the first EV practitioner examination in Great Britain. Another milestone has been reached in equipping our project managers with the knowledge and skills they need to deliver – on time, to budget – and to keep repeating it.

The 2012 Olympics were held in venues across Great Britain, built and delivered with earned value at their very core. At all times we knew what we needed to do, as well as when and how much. By adopting this technique, this herculean task was not only delivered on time but also gave back over £950 million pounds of taxpayers' money.

As part of the learning legacy of the Games we concluded that the project was a success due in large part to a back-to-basics approach. Doing the right things right.

If we can deliver projects in this way – so can you. Earned value remains the tool of choice, an internationally recognised standard framework for considering, controlling, informing and managing projects.

Earned value projects may not always win gold but its use helps you do the best you can. An Olympic ideal for us all in our lives.

Sir John Armitt
Chairman, Olympic Delivery Authority

Acknowledgements

The Earned Value Management Handbook was developed by a sub-group of the APM Planning, Monitoring and Control (PMC) SIG with contributions from Clive Bolton, Jenn Browne, Mike Burke, Alan Bye, Caroline Clarke, Jonathan Crone, Alex Davis, John Flaherty, Ewan Glen, Guy Hindley, Stephen Jones, Paul Kidston, Deborah Perrin, Claire Purser, Breda Ryan and Steve Wake.

The APM PMC SIG is most grateful to BAE Systems, BMT HiQSigma, Defence Equipment and Support (DE&S) and Sellafield Ltd who have made documents and images available to the SIG to assist in producing this work.

The review and testing of this handbook has been conducted by the PMC SIG members and volunteers from a number of industry sectors – with positive feedback so far.

The authors would like to thank everyone for their help in making the Earned Value Management Handbook a reality.

Purpose

The content of this document identifies the scope of Earned Value Management (EVM) knowledge as understood by the APM Planning, Monitoring and Control (PMC) Specific Interest Group (SIG). This knowledge was compiled and discussed in a series of working sessions and reviews commencing in October 2010 and concluding, for publication purposes, in August 2011.

It provides reference guidance for practitioners and students along with the study material required for both the Foundation and Practitioner exams.

1 Introduction

EVM is a good practice approach used for the planning, management and control of projects and programmes. These can range from large programmes to relatively small, internal company projects. The approach supports the establishment of a baseline project plan, and then the management of cost and schedule performance to that plan in an integrated way. The *Earned Value Management: APM Guidelines* (2008) provide guidance on the approach at a foundation level. This publication provides guidance at both the Foundation and the Practitioner level.

EV qualifications are currently offered at two levels: Foundation and Practitioner.

The text of this publication is structured according to the EVM Syllabus May 2011 (APM Group). The syllabus follows the EV process originally detailed in the *Earned Value Management: APM Guidelines*. Adherence to this structure makes this publication a useful study guide and a source of reference.

The primary purpose of the syllabus is to provide a basis for the accreditation of people involved with earned value. It documents the learning outcomes related to the use of earned value and describes the requirements a candidate is expected to meet to demonstrate that these learning outcomes have been achieved at each qualification level.

Foundation level

This level provides information and knowledge for individuals who have an understanding of the *Earned Value Management: APM Guidelines (APM, 2008)*, and who are currently actively involved, or are likely to be actively involved, in an earned value project environment. It allows them to contribute to the formal process of earned value management.

NB: Material relating to Foundation level knowledge and extracted from the *Earned Value Management: APM Guidelines* is shown in blue.

Practitioner level

This level provides information and knowledge for individuals who have worked, and are working, in an earned value management environment and have done so for a period of two years. This audience will include a wide range of people working on earned value based projects including project managers, control account managers, and project planners and project analysts.

A practitioner has achieved sufficient understanding of the theory and application of earned value management to allow them to work successfully in an earned value management environment. They should be capable of applying the tools and techniques independently but will have a team around them and advice and support available as required. A successful practitioner should, with suitable direction, be able to start applying the method to a real project but may not be sufficiently skilled to do this appropriately for all situations.

2 Overview

2.1 The types of project where earned value may be applied

Earned Value Management: APM Guidelines can be applied to projects of varying size, scope and duration to ensure that the EVM process is operated in a consistent manner across all implementing teams. Each implementing project should take into account:

- project specific requirements;

- customer requirements;

- lessons learnt from previous projects;

- IT toolset requirements;

- impact on resources and infrastructure.

Project managers should ensure that progress and performance measurements are realistic and are in accordance with this guide.

2.2 The definition of earned value

Earned value management is a project control process based on a structured approach to planning, cost collection and performance measurement. It facilitates the integration of project scope, time and cost objectives and the establishment of a baseline plan for performance measurement (Association for Project Management, 2006).

The establishment of a performance measurement baseline (PMB) is essential to conducting successful EVM and consists of:

- defined scope and assumptions;

- activities scheduled in logical sequence;

- resources/costs (labour and materials) to be time-phased in line with the schedule.

We need to know:

- what the status of the plan is;

- what the project has achieved;

- what has been spent to date.

2.3 The purpose of earned value

Earned value helps us manage by:

- providing data to enable objective measurement of project status;

- providing a basis for estimating final cost;

- predicting when the project will be complete;

- supporting the effective management of resources;

- providing a means of managing and controlling change.

Informed and effective decision making is enabled by knowing:

- what has been achieved of the plan;

- what it has cost to achieve the planned work;

- if the work achieved is costing more or less than was planned;

- if the project is ahead of or behind the planned schedule.

Good planning leads to good project execution and good management information. Poor planning can lead to poor execution and poor EVM information. The plan must be maintained in accordance with authorised project changes. EVM will accurately show deviations from the plan, but it may not be immediately evident that a flawed plan is being tracked.

EVM is about establishing and managing goals throughout the life of a project. It comprises the following:

- definition and authorisation of the contract scope of work;

- development of a 'baseline' against which cost, schedule and technical performance can be measured;

- objective performance measurement;

- variance analysis and corrective action reporting;

- disciplined and timely incorporation of 'baseline' changes.

An earned value management system (EVMS) will provide the following:

- verifiable status reports;

- clear objective analysis;

- considered reasoning;

- accountability in the decision-making process;

- awareness of impact on the schedule and cost across the project;

- visibility of results.

A system should be created that will enable the measurement of the four key data elements essential to EVMS, namely:

1. The budgeted cost of work scheduled (BCWS) or planned value (PV) – i.e. what we are going to do, the plan: the schedule for the expenditure of budgeted resources as necessary to meet project scope and schedule objectives. It is important to understand that BCWS is a *schedule*, stated in the value of work to be performed, and is therefore a basis for both time and cost assessment of the progress on a project.

2. The actual cost of work performed (ACWP) or actual cost (AC) – i.e. what the work achieved actually cost.

3. The budgeted cost of work performed (BCWP) or earned value (EV) – i.e. what the amount of work achieved should have cost, according to the planned budget: the *earned value* for the work actually achieved.

4. The estimate at completion (EAC) of the project. This is the ACWP to date, plus the most knowledgeable estimate of remaining requirements, scope, schedule and cost.

Guidelines exist for companies to use in establishing and applying an EVMS. These guidelines are expressed in fundamental terms and provide flexibility for each company to optimise its system, and be fully accountable for the effectiveness of its usage. These guidelines (or criteria) are recognised as an international standard. An EVMS that is developed to meet the intent of the criteria will allow key stakeholders, notably customers and shareholders, to gain confidence that projects are being managed and resources deployed in an effective and consistent manner against a recognised standard.

2.3.1 What are the benefits?

Figure 1 shows the traditional budget vs. actual graph. It is traditionally used to compare budget with actual spend.

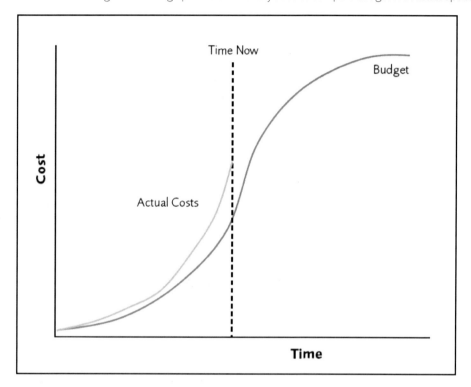

Figure 1: Budget vs actual graph
Taken from the *Earned Value Management: APM Guidelines* (2008)

The graph does not show:

- if the project is ahead of or behind schedule;

- if the project is truly over- or under-spending;

- if the project is getting value for money;

- if money has been spent on the right things;

- if the problems are over or have only just begun.

The graph shown in Figure 2 is similar to the previous graph except that a measure of performance (or status value) has been included. The line included is the *earned value* or *achievement* line. This additional line represents the proportion of the budget that has actually been achieved.

Figure 2 indicates the following additional information:

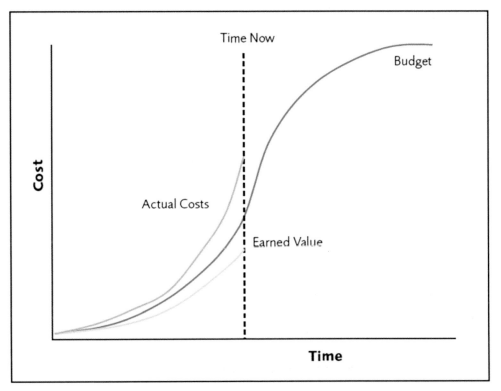

Figure 2: Budget vs actual plus earned value graph
Taken from *Earned Value Management: APM Guidelines* (2008)

- the project is underachieving because the amount (value) of work completed (earned value) is less than that scheduled;

- the project is overspent because the cost of the work completed is greater than the budgeted cost of work completed (earned value);

- the cost performance is actually worse than was indicated on the traditional chart because it shows an over-expenditure coupled with underachievement of planned work scope;

- the project is spending money inefficiently, as it is costing more to achieve progress than planned. The cost problems do not appear to be contained, since the slope of the actual cost line is greater that the budgeted cost line; this indicates that the overspend is going to increase, even though the earned value line does look like it will intersect the budget cost line some time in the future. While schedule recovery may yet be possible, the cost impact is unlikely to be recovered.

2.3.2 Using performance measurements

Any measurements of performance are *indicators* of the efficiency or performance of a project. As such, they should be used as *one* of the many criteria on which project managers should base their decisions, having interpreted the information and placed it in context.

Performance measurements indicate where shortfalls are occurring or likely to occur. These can be used to identify where extra resources, management actions or other support are required in order to overcome problems. They are early indicators of problems and give pointers as to what might happen to the project if actions are not taken.

2.4 Common acronyms and their meanings

The budgeted cost of work scheduled (BCWS) or planned value (PV)
This is the detail of the plan, what is being done, and includes the schedule for the expenditure of budgeted resources as necessary to meet project scope and schedule objectives. It is important to understand that the BCWS is a schedule, stated in the value of work to be performed, and is therefore a basis for both the time and cost assessment of the progress of a project.

The actual cost of work performed (ACWP) or actual cost (AC)
This is what the work achieved actually cost.

The budgeted cost of work performed (BCWP) or Earned Value (EV)
This is what the amount of work achieved should have cost, according to the planned budget.

The estimate at completion (EAC) of the project
This is the ACWP to date, plus the most knowledgeable estimate of the remaining requirements, scope, schedule and cost.

Please also refer to earned value abbreviations and acronyms on page 167.

2.5 Designing an earned value implementation for a specific organisation and project

Considerations

An Earned Value Management System (EVMS) is a type of project control system. All organisations managing projects have an identifiable project control system.

A set of 32 criteria describe the characteristics of an EVMS. The criteria concept does not describe a system but it is intended to state the qualities and operational considerations of a project control system, using earned value management without permitting system-level characteristics.

It is expected that appropriate adherence to the criteria will allow key stakeholders, notably customers and shareholders, to gain confidence that projects are being managed and resources deployed in an effective manner.

The criteria require project control systems to provide data which:

* provides timely and reliable information about work progress;
* properly relates cost, schedule and technical achievement;
* supplies managers with information at a practical level of summarisation.

An agreed version or alternative to the 32 criteria may be used as the point of comparison or definition of the project control system, for example, *The Earned Value Management Compass (APM, 2010)*.

* The criteria are internationally recognised and contained in ANSI-748 EVMS.
* The criteria are also contained in APM Guidelines for earned value.
* The ANSI-748 and APM guidelines are reciprocal.
* The criteria describe the characteristics that an EVMS project control system must be able to demonstrate from zero to full compliance against each criterion.
* The criteria are not prescriptive.
* The project control system meets the criteria in terms of their intent.
* There may be many ways to show that the intent of a criterion is being met.
* The different possible ways for meeting a criterion allow for flexibility in system design.
* Each EVMS can be different in how it satisfies a criterion, and the degree to which it satisfies a criterion.
* Any project control system can be compared with the criteria and rated for compliance whether earned value is being used or not.
* The degree of compliance determines how efficiently and effectively earned value data can be generated from the project control system.
* The degree of compliance does not of itself determine how well the needs of the project and its stakeholders are being met.
* The degree of compliance can be used by management to compare the actual project control system with the expected project control system.
* A mismatch between the actual and expected project control system will affect project performance.
* The mismatch may be accepted by management or result in authorised work to be undertaken to narrow or close the mismatch.
* The design of an EVMS is a combination of what is required, desirable and achievable.

Inputs

* Project control system description (verified actual or theoretical).

- 32 EVMS criteria description.
- Audit method.
- Audit timetable.
- Organisation project control standard.
- Contracts or agreements with EVMS requirements.

Method

- *The Earned Value Management Compass* (APM, 2010).

Outputs

- Audit report of EVMS compliance.
- Change plan (including a risk-assessed and costed schedule) to address the findings of the audit to achieve the desired project control system design, if required.

2.6 The factors to be taken into account when designing an earned value implementation

The ultimate aim of an earned value implementation is to design a process or system that provides integrated, reliable management information that accurately reflects the current status of projects. It should also predict expected project outcomes based on accurate and up to date progress data. This will be compromised if the design is too bureaucratic, under resourced or isolated from day to day management, or if the outcome is not used.

The resources provided to the implementation team should correlate with the expectations of the implementation sponsors in terms of:

- time;
- finances;
- team members;
- senior management support.

It will be essential to fully understand these expectations so that they can be managed and the implementation plan kept both realistic and achievable.

The implementation of an EVMS is in the form of a change programme. The change programme moves the existing project control system from its current state towards the required level of EVMS.

The change programme for achieving an EVMS is not the same as the everyday operation of the EVMS, when it is used to control projects, programmes and portfolios.

When an organisation has made the decision to implement earned value, there are factors to be considered in the design of the implementation as a whole, both at organisational level and for individual projects.

2.6.1 Why is EV being implemented?

Customer demand: the customer may have included a contractual requirement for the application of earned value in some form (regular reporting, compliance with standards, payment terms based on EV performance). This may direct certain reporting requirements and levels of visibility and traceability of data that will need to be incorporated within the design.

Senior management directive: senior members of the organisation may have stated that earned value is to be applied to all projects fulfilling identified criteria (value, level of complexity and degree of risk, for example, in terms of the technical and financial aspects as well as the schedule). Again this may drive reporting requirements.

Individual project manager requirement: if an individual project manager has requested that EV be implemented on their project, the level of investment available will be small compared with a company-wide or customer-driven requirement, due to the more limited payback potential from a single project.

2.6.2 The requirements that the earned value implementation will be expected to meet

2.6.2.1 The EVMS mandate

It is good practice to record the rationale supporting the decision to implement an EVMS. The mandate can be revisited before, during and after completion of the implementation to check, compare and clarify assumptions and achievements.

The mandate should be presented in the form of a business case and should set out the justification and strategic rationale for the project. It also provides a framework for informed decision-making in project planning and management and its subsequent benefits realisation. The mandate's foundation is an evidence-based evaluation of the benefit, costs and risk of a solution against a need, problem or opportunity identified by the sponsor and approved by the funding organisation.

The contents of the business case should include:

* the reason for the project;
* a high-level description of the project scope;
* the contractual obligations;
* an evaluation of all options, including the 'do nothing' option;
* the direct and indirect benefits;
* any risks (of all options including the 'do nothing' option);
* the estimated costs;
* the target schedule;
* the investment appraisal;
* the assumptions made;
* the identified constraints;
* any dependencies;
* the project success criteria;
* the impact on business as usual.

Considerations

The implementation of the EVMS should be designed to make use of existing, reliable and organisation-wide accepted processes or systems.

The factors to be considered in the implementation design focus on two fundamental questions:

1. What do I need?
2. What have I got?

The gaps between the two can then be identified and the methods for closing each gap planned effectively. The plan to close the gaps should consider:

- timescales;
- people;
- money.

There are many other elements and areas that will require consideration when looking at the EVM implementation design. One of the major factors will be set-up costs and the time burden of undertaking the implementation, which can include:

- the process and system design and creation (both current and target states);
- EVM expertise – own or procured?
- The process and system developers' expertise;
- accommodation;
- equipment;
- administration;
- training needs of the project team, PmO, etc.;
- training and coaching needs of the supporting areas;
- integration and handover.

The business as usual running costs and time burden can include:

- system maintenance;
- PSO support – cost and schedule maintenance, analysis and reporting;
- update collection;
- the continued coaching of supporting areas.

2.6.3 Factors for the assessment of existing or start-up project control systems

2.6.3.1 EVM foundations

The attributes below are reproduced directly from *The Earned Value Management Compass* (APM, 2010).

Attribute 1 – Earned value management competencies

Aim: To ensure that the project team has the appropriate competencies to implement and manage using an EVMS.

Reason: EVM is often a new process to a project or business and requires appropriate training and education for its implementation to be a success. The implementation and operation of an EVM system can be a complex exercise and can be facilitated by the use of experienced resources.

Guidance information
It is important that training and support are provided during EVM implementation and that ongoing training is also available. The team members should be trained in EVM techniques appropriate to their role within the project team.

Implementation of EVM is best facilitated by using resources with previous implementation experience. Learned experience from other projects is also a valuable source of information.

Attribute 2 – Sponsorship

Aim: To ensure that there is clear and visible EVM sponsorship for the project from within the delivery organisation.

Reason: It is important that the implementation and execution of EVM is sponsored at an appropriate level within the project/ organisation to ensure high level management support.

Guidance information
The introduction of EVM may cause the need for a significant cultural change, which must be led with senior management support and sponsorship. This should be communicated throughout the entire project structure.

The understanding and commitment of the entire project team and organisational functional areas is vital for success. Therefore there is a need for comprehensive communication outlining the nature of EVM along with the aims and objectives of the implementation.

2.6.3.2 EVM basics

Attribute 3 – Project-level authorisation

Aim: To ensure that the project has been given appropriate approval and authority to proceed.

Reason: The project should be formally approved by the responsible organisation. This approval should indicate the overall budget available and assign delivery responsibility/authority onto the key individuals within the project team. It should also indicate the sponsor within the organisation.

Guidance information
Prior to commencing the project work, the approval authority should formally sanction the project to proceed and assign the required level of responsibility, authority and accountability (RAA) to the project manager. To further delegate this RAA to the team delivering the project, a responsibility assignment matrix (RAM) is used.
The RAM process is principally concerned with defining the work to be done, as a work breakdown structure (WBS), and assigning that work to specific parts of the project's organisation via the organisational breakdown structure (OBS). The WBS and OBS should be aligned and combined to produce a concise RAM.

Within the RAM, each element of work is assigned to an organisational element and a single person within the organisation. This is regarded as an individual control account (CA). Each control account will be owned by a control account manager (CAM) and will contain lower level, detailed work packages (or near-term work) and also summarised PPs (or far-term work).

Attribute 4 – Work definition

Aim: To ensure that the full scope of work associated with the project has been broken into manageable elements in a manner that supports performance reporting.

Reason: The project scope of work should be broken into manageable elements in a manner that supports the delivery of work and performance reporting. Failure to break down work appropriately can lead to difficulties with assigning a single point of accountability for delivery of the work, and can also lead to confusing, conflicting and sometimes incomplete performance data.

Guidance information

All work that will be performed under the contract must be formally authorised and defined within the framework of a logical breakdown of work, normally via a work breakdown structure (WBS), and will be assigned to individuals responsible for undertaking that work.

The WBS provides a common management framework for all project activities, and there must only be one WBS for any single contract. The WBS will be cross-referenced with the contract statement of work or a statement of requirements to ensure the full scope of work has been covered.

The level to which a WBS is broken down depends on the complexity of the contract and the level of detail required for its effective management. Essentially, the WBS should continue until all contract requirements and business requirements can be attributed to meaningful work packages.

In any project, the WBS is of critical importance because it defines not only how the work of the project is broken down, but also provides the framework for collecting actual costs, reporting progress and measuring achievement.

Attribute 5 – Detail work authorisation and budget assignment

Aim: To ensure that all distributed work has an associated budget, has been assigned to an individual with delivery responsibility, and that all work is authorised before it commences.

Reason: Every package of work within the WBS should be assigned an agreed budget for its completion. This should be commensurate with the scope of work to be delivered, for example it should be sufficient to cover labour, material and other direct costs that will be incurred while delivering the work. Before work commences, the associated budget and schedule must be authorised to indicate approval to proceed (typically this would open associated cost booking numbers).

Guidance information

The detail work authorisation and budget assignment process ensures that every package of work within the WBS is assigned an agreed budget for its completion. This is part of the formal authorisation process that allows work to commence against the agreed schedule baseline for each control account (CA) – and therefore the project as a whole. These budgets may consist of a labour element (resources) and/or materials element and will be assigned to all WPs and PPs. However, it is recommended that the different cost types should be kept in separate WPs/PPs where possible.

To manage the completion of work against WPs they will usually only be opened when they have been formally authorised (typically when they are due to commence within the next few months) and will be closed when they are completed. This also helps to ensure that full control is maintained over the WP and no work is completed against it, either before it is authorised or after it has been deemed to be complete and full earned value claimed.

Attribute 6 – Responsibility and accountability

Aim: To ensure that identified staff within the project team have appropriately delegated and documented responsibilities and accountabilities and that these have been communicated.

Reason: It is important that all project staff are clear on what they are responsible for delivering, and that they have the necessary authority to fulfil their roles and responsibilities. While achieving this, it is also crucial that accountability rests with single individuals.

Guidance information

The project team (including control account managers) have responsibility for the delivery of the project. It is essential that individuals within the project have a clear definition and understanding of their terms of reference and that these are clearly understood by those within the project and the associated functional organisational areas.

A control account manager (CAM) has management responsibility for ensuring that the defined scope of work for a control account is achieved to the set budget, timescale and quality standards. The CAM manages the CA as a contract between themselves and the project manager/project director.

Typical CAM terms of reference are for someone:

* who is accountable for ensuring that the defined scope of work for a discrete control account is achieved to budget and timescales; with the delegated authority to manage the deployment and mix of resources required to achieve budget and timescales;

* who is empowered to manage the internal contract between the project and the organisation performing the work;

* who is experienced in project delivery/management and can strike the balance between technical and business requirements;

* who can demonstrate adequate knowledge, commitment and ownership of their control accounts.

Attribute 7 – Material management

Aim: To ensure that the material budget is included in the EVMS in order to support accurate performance reporting.

Reason: To establish the complete project budget and enable material performance management, it is essential to ensure that the material elements are contained within the performance measurement baseline (PMB).

Guidance information
The management of purchased materials/services covers the processes and activities that directly affect the purchase of bill of material items or services from external suppliers. These elements should all be captured in the EVMS with appropriate progress measurement and actual cost collection techniques.

Attribute 8 – Basis of estimate

Aim: To ensure that the rationale for producing the estimates that underpin the budget and schedule data are contained in a formal document.

Reason: The basis of estimate (BoE), accompanied with related assumptions, ensures that the project manager/team can demonstrate how both the budget and schedule were developed. It aids future reviews of the budget, which is particularly important if the staff involved in their original development are no longer available.

Guidance information

In reviewing this area it is important to understand the CAM's role in formulating the proposal estimate/budget for the effort. A number of questions should be asked:

- How did they arrive at the proposed estimates?
- Are there backup worksheets to give more detail?
- Was there a negotiation process for the budgets after the contract was awarded?
- Is the budget adequate and what risks are there in achieving the work within budget?

The data justifying the responses to these questions should be formally documented in the BoE file.

Attribute 9 – Management reserve (cost and schedule)

Aim: To ensure that management reserve is identified, documented and approved, and is subject to formal change approval when drawn upon by the project team.

Reason: Projects should have a separately identified management reserve budget that can be used for unplanned scope. The management reserve (MR) budget will usually be sized based on the risk exposure of the project as represented in the risk register.

Guidance information

The MR is set aside for project management control purposes only. It is not a contingency that can be eliminated by the customer during subsequent negotiations, nor can it be used by the customer to absorb the cost of contract changes.

MR is derived during the budgeting process. It is held separately for future allocation to control accounts (using the project change process) and will be used, if required, to cover increased work-scope requirements for unforeseen changes that fall within the overall scope of the contract. For more details, please see *Interfacing Risk and Earned Value Management* (APM, 2008) on this subject.

Attribute 10 – Supplier budget integration

Aim: To ensure that the supplier's budget is included in the EVMS to support accurate performance reporting.

Reason: To establish the complete project budget and enable supplier performance management, it is essential to ensure that the supplier budget elements are contained within the performance measurement baseline.

Guidance information

The nature of budget integration will depend on the earned value approach prescribed for the supplier. This could be:

- full EVM requirements flowed down to the supplier to report budgeted cost for work performed (BCWP);
- actual cost of work performed (ACWP) periodically;
- milestone based EV measurement where a milestone payment plan linked to physical progress is agreed with the supplier and this forms the BCWS;
- a BCWS is established based on the planned receipt of commodities and consumables.

The approach defined will depend on the nature of the item being procured, the criticality and the risks/opportunities. Where full EVM is flowed down to the supplier, the contract should clearly define the requirement.

For more guidance on the selection of the best approach please refer to *Earned Value Management: APM Guidelines (APM, 2008)*.

Attribute 11 – Schedule structure and content

Aim: To ensure that there is a robust, time-phased, logically-linked set of activities and milestones that show how products/outputs will be delivered.

Reason: The critical objective for any project is the delivery of the product to time, specification and cost. As such, a schedule or suite of schedules needs to be created to display the logic, durations and interdependencies of all project activities.

Guidance information
The schedule should cover all work-scope and will include all master milestones, for example, payment milestones, contract deliverables and key programme milestones. There will be a clear link between the established CAs and WPs created within the EVM system and the activities within the schedule.

The schedule should enable the critical path to be clearly visible. Supplier schedules should be integrated at a level of detail dependent on the type of scope or service being purchased. The amount of detail within the schedule will be dependent on the nature and scale of the project. See Attribute 14 on page 23.

Attribute 12 – Schedule resource allocation

Aim: To ensure that the schedule is fully resourced and that resource planning is undertaken.

Reason: The schedule should be resourced with the amount and type of resources required to deliver the project. This is usually done using a resource breakdown structure (RBS) to identify the skill types within an organisation. Resource levelling should be conducted to ensure that the resources required to deliver the project are available when required.

Guidance information
The schedule resource requirements should be understood within the context of the wider resource requirements of the organisation. Use of the schedule should allow proactive, flexible resource management to optimise the utilisation of the workforce within an organisation.

Attribute 13 – Objectivity of EV progress assessment

Aim: To ensure that appropriate earned value techniques (EVT) are applied.

Reason: To accurately assess progress it is important to assign the most appropriate EVTs to activities/work packages. Without this, the performance reported may fail to reflect the actual performance achieved.

Guidance information
The EVT is the technique used to measure achievement, also known as the budgeted cost of work performed BCWP or EV. The optimum EVT must be assigned to individual work packages. The vast majority of work packages on a project should be a

discrete type as these provide the most objective measure of the value of in progress work.

The EVT chosen must best represent the effort required to accomplish the work in the project and provide the most appropriate method for planning, scheduling and evaluating performance. Work packages should be identified as one of three types:

1. **discrete tasks** – that have a specific end product or result;
2. **apportioned** – factored effort that can be directly related to other identified discrete tasks;
3. **level of effort** (LoE) – support/management type of work which does not result in a final product – performance/achievement cannot be measured since there is no tangible output.

The EVTs for each WP on a project should be documented, with the WBS structured so that the LoE on a project can be accurately reported.

Attribute 14 – Supplier schedule integration

Aim: To ensure that project schedules reflect supplier activities and deliverables, which in turn provide visibility of the interaction between the schedules of all parties.

Reason: To enable supplier progress tracking and to fully understand the interdependencies, it is essential to ensure that the supplier schedules are contained within the project master schedule.

Guidance information
The way sub-contractor effort is integrated into the baseline will differ according to its importance to the project. The distinction between major and minor sub-contractor should be based upon factors such as equipment value, criticality, or risk to the project (e.g. single source supply) and/or whether they are an off-the-shelf supplier or not.

It is essential to ensure that sub-contractors' schedules are represented within the project master schedule to an appropriate level of detail, and that there is a process for reporting and managing the sub-contracted effort. The requirements for sub-contractor schedule provision and reporting should be defined in their contract.
In the event of progress payments being used, a definition of the method of validating the supplier's performance should be recorded in the purchase order (or contract).

Schedules on a major project can be very large and complex; decisions have to be taken regarding the level of detail to be incorporated into the project's master schedule. If there is too much detail, the maintenance of the plan becomes a burdensome overhead, while insufficient detail can make the exact status of the project difficult to ascertain.

It is usually the key deliverables that need to be monitored and controlled by the contractor. The focus of supplier schedules is typically:

- payment milestones (ideally one per period);
- key events and/or way points (identified by period where possible);
- deliverables into the contractor;
- deliverables to other sub-contractors (interface milestones).

If a milestone-based EVM is being used, identified milestones will be allocated a budget/resource, based on the agreed payment to the sub-contractor. This will ideally follow the agreed payment profile (please refer to Attribute 10 – Supplier budget integration on page 21). Budgeted milestones will be time-phased to create a BCWS for the sub-contractor.

Attribute 15 – Process documentation and consistency of application

Aim: To ensure that the EVM processes are formally described and documented.

Reason: Documented processes should be communicated to all relevant stakeholders to ensure consistent understanding and application.

Guidance information

Formal process documentation should be created and be in operational use for all the EVM processes to an appropriate level of detail. It is important to document processes and procedures to enable the continued operation of the process as new people join the project.

Where generic EVM processes are in use they may be tailored with guidelines to meet specific local requirements. These could be in the form of local project/process instructions for different projects. A pragmatic balance should be reached between any internal procedures and external contract-specified standards. Any local project instructions are under configuration control.

2.6.3.3 Execute EVM

Attribute 16 – Actual cost collection

Aim: To ensure the costs are collected at a level appropriate for performance reporting and that they can be reconciled with the accounting system.

Reason: It is important to ensure the accuracy of cost collection and ensure that it is related to the correct activity within the activity/work package. Without this information the cost of the authorised work will not be fully understood and reported.

Guidance information

The accounting processes ensure that complete and accurate cost information is collected in a timely manner. This enables the transfer of actual cost information into the project control system's cost reporting tool (by period).

Costs will be associated with the planned work and will be recorded at activity, WP or CA level, and will be rolled-up to provide actual costs across the control account(s) and at the summary project level. The creation of booking or charge numbers, matched to the discrete aspects of the WBS, will also make it possible to measure progress and achievements in a meaningful manner (against the baseline plan). This in turn facilitates effective financial control of the project by enabling the organisation to identify the full cost associated with the project activity. Through linkage with the recording of progress against tasks, the estimated costs at completion for the planned work remaining can be identified.

Direct costs are accumulated as labour-man hours and non-labour pounds against the relevant booking or charge numbers. Across the project, the project control system's source collection systems will collect information and feed it into the cost ledger. The appropriate charging rates will be applied to labour hours to give a complete picture of the actual cost of the work performed. Indirect costs should also be captured at a level appropriate to allow their effective management.

Once the actual spend is available, all CAMs are responsible for verifying that they are both accurate and a true reflection of the actual costs of performing the work within that period.
Material costs should also be collected in the same period as the EV is claimed. This may require the use of estimated actuals or accruals. A process to check the accuracy of the actual costs should be developed and performed periodically, and any corrections to actual costs should be appropriately documented.

If there are differences between the finance systems and the EVMS it should be possible to identify and determine the reason for the differences.

Attribute 17 – Schedule progress and control

Aim: To ensure that the schedule is updated and analysed to capture progress and determine the performance against the baseline, enabling informed management actions.

Reason: Establishing earned value performance requires the schedule progress to be captured on a periodic basis.

Guidance information
Every period, schedule progress and achievement (i.e. EV) is collected and processed. Schedule variances against the baseline should be determined and reported. Critical path analysis of the current schedule and baseline schedule should be performed. Float should also be determined. As a result of the analysis information, management actions (corrective actions) are determined and implemented.

Schedule progress and control will also allow the impact on current resource plans to be evaluated and an estimate to completion (EAC) can be generated for the remaining work.

Attribute 18 – Data integrity

Aim: To ensure that data is checked for accuracy.

Reason: To provide confidence that it is accurate enough to support management decisions.

Guidance information
Checking processes should be in place to identify errors in the EVM data set. Any adjustments required must be to correct errors. Any financial transfers that are required should be made in the period following the error. Genuine cost variances should not be disguised through this process.

Attribute 19 – Estimate at completion

Aim: To ensure that the project generates a valid estimate at completion (EAC) including cost and schedule.

Reason: The EAC provides an indication of the final funding requirements for the project, in addition to the likely completion date. (See also Attribute 17 – Schedule progress and control above.

Guidance information
There are two main types of EAC:

- a CAM estimate* of the resources required to complete the work package over time;
- independent estimate based upon standard EV calculations.

*a CAM estimate is typically done by determining the estimate to completion (ETC) for each work package and adding it to the actual cost to date to produce the EAC.

When establishing an ETC the following aspects should be considered:

- past performance (efficiency) and trends;
- costs incurred to date;
- commitments placed (to date and potential future);
- required efficiency to 'recover' variances;
- technical assessment of remaining activities;
- anticipated future efficiency (should relate to past performance);
- forecast of schedule (time) to complete activity;
- associated risks with remaining activity;
- future economic conditions, for example, rate changes, escalation indices and revised supplier contracts;
- previous ETC trends.

There is a range of standard independent estimates at completion (IEAC) calculation formulae that can be used to identify the potential project out-turn based upon performance to date. These are outlined in the *Earned Value Management: APM Guidelines (APM, 2008)*.

The control account manager's EAC should be compared with the standard IEAC calculations that are based on previous performance. This will provide a check on how realistic they are.

Attribute 20 – Supplier management and reporting

Aim: To ensure that supplier performance reporting is aligned with the requirements of the project, to enable effective supplier management.

Reason: Significant areas of projects are often managed and delivered by suppliers. It is important that these suppliers report relevant, agreed progress information periodically.

Guidance information
Sub-contractors should provide a periodic progress report which contains information relevant to the nature of the procurement (refer to Attribute 14 – Supplier schedule integration on page 23). It is important that there is verification of the accuracy of the supplier information. This may be achieved during performance reviews with the supplier or by physical onsite verification.

Attribute 21 – Risk and opportunity management

Aim: To ensure that there is alignment between the risk management and EVM processes.

Reason: The risk management processes within a project overlap with the EVM processes, particularly around unplanned work-scope and the EAC.

Guidance information
Risk and opportunity management is an integral part of EVM and is concerned with managing threats to the baseline. The management of opportunity is focused on improving performance against the baseline.

EV and risk and opportunity management are fully integrated into the project team's management and control processes, and regular reviews which seek to maintain or improve this position are undertaken. Approved and budgeted risk mitigation or opportunity realisation activities should be included in the baseline project master schedule. The consumption of management reserve should be tracked in relation to the remaining risk exposure of the project. This is equally applicable to funds and schedule reserve.

Attribute 22 – Baseline change management

Aim: To ensure that changes to the PMB are carried out in a timely and controlled manner.

Reason: The baseline should contain the complete, agreed scope of work. As projects progress change is inevitable; the introduction of these changes into the baseline should be controlled.

Guidance information

To ensure that the project is managed in a controlled manner it is important that all changes are embodied into the PMB in a controlled and documented manner. Change management addresses the controlled process where formal change, internal re-planning and adjustments (past, present and future) to information are incorporated.

The baseline change process exists in order to ensure all requests for change are recorded, progressed and tracked in a timely manner. Change can be requested through four sources:

1. the project;
2. CAM;
3. customer;
4. sub-contractor.

Where there is an impact on the baseline, the associated CAM must define the effect on the work scope, schedule, budget and product configuration. The level of authority for approving PMB changes must be clearly defined in either the project management plan or a project control plan, and any changes that are approved must be implemented within the PMB in a timely manner. Budgets should not be transferred without corresponding work scope. Change should also not be used to remedy or hide poor performance.

Attribute 23 – Senior management usage

Aim: To ensure that EVM information is available for senior management, to inform decision making during project, programme and portfolio reviews.

Reason: Senior management must have a basic understanding of EVM to be able to interpret the data they receive. They may also need to be involved in providing project direction should variances become significant.

Guidance information

Adopting the principle of management by exception, there may be times when senior management needs to become involved in the project decision-making process. It is important that the senior management team has a clear understanding of EVM in project management and can interpret the information provided.

Attribute 24 – Customer involvement

Aim: To ensure EVM is operated in a manner that allows customer involvement.

Reason: To enable EVM to be used in an open and transparent manner facilitating the required level of customer involvement.

Guidance information
The customer is typically the client or organisation that is funding the project.

The nature of customer involvement may be largely shaped by whether the customer has stated the requirement for EVM within the contract or if the project is using EVM as part of its standard company policy. If the customer has specified EVM, the expectation is that they have an active interest and would receive the relevant EVM reports. They would typically be involved in the decision-making process and be party to recovery planning.

2.6.3.4 EVM goal

Attribute 25 – EVM as a decision support tool

Aim: To ensure that EVM information forms a key component of project performance management reviews. It provides the vision on the future direction of the project, giving the project manager the opportunity (where appropriate) to provide corrective actions to re-direct the project to enable it to meet its aims.

Reason: The value provided by EVM is achieved by using the data to make informed decisions. Producing EV data but not linking this to the decision-making process does not meet the aims of the process and the true value of EVM will not be evident.

INPUTS	PROCESS	OUTPUTS
• Mandate. • Standards and guidelines. • Current project controls, system description and processes. • Existing resources – budget and people. • Gap analysis. • Stakeholder analysis. • Readiness review. • EV maturity review – Earned Value Management Compass (APM, 2010). • Existing project controls expertise.	The Earned Value Management Compass (APM, 2010).	• Project controls system description. • Earned Value system implementation plan. • Defined change programme. • Benefits map. • Defined business case for the change required.

Table 1: Table showing the outputs as a result of using the *Earned Value Management Compass* (APM, 2010)

2.7 Evaluating the project controls environment in an organisation

The main areas requiring assessment are:

- the contract;
- business case;
- establishing the plan;
- agreeing the baseline;
- collecting progress;
- engaging project stakeholders;
- applying governance to the process;
- reporting variances;
- use of the data;
- senior management buy-in and support for the process.

The more mature the current project controls environment, the greater the benefits of EVM reporting to the organisation. The input data should be more readily available and the output data will be more likely to be used in management decision making at all levels of the project and organisation.

2.8 Defining the target level of earned value implementation for the size, complexity, risk and importance of a specific project

A review is conducted using a maturity grid, for example the *Earned Value Management Compass (APM, 2010)*, outlining performance levels against 25 attributes of an EVM system. A target standard should be established for the project or projects within an organisation at the outset, and the maturity at the time of review should be related to this target standard.

The target standard to be achieved should be agreed by a customer of the project or within an organisation, and it is for individual project teams/organisations to set their target standards. However, customers who require full ANSI 748 compliance are unlikely to be satisfied with less than full compliance.

Where an organisation doesn't implement full EVM, as outlined in ANSI 748, the maturity level achieved will be reduced, with the possibility that several of the products identified will not be available. This however, may be appropriate for that particular organisation.

The assessment process allows the project's strengths and weaknesses to be identified and should culminate in planned improvement actions which are then monitored for progress.

The frequency of reviews is a decision for the project team or organisation.

2.8.1 What are the benefits?

Using the *Earned Value Management Compass* (APM, 2010) maturity framework for assessment delivers a range of benefits, including:

* identifying the organisation's strengths and weaknesses;
* providing a highly structured, fact-based approach to identifying and assessing the project and measuring progress periodically;
* creating a common language and conceptual framework for managing and improving EVM on the project and, if applicable, projects within the organisation;
* educating people in the project on the fundamental elements of EVM and how they relate to roles and responsibilities;
* involving people at all levels in process improvement; ranking EVM project maturity within an organisation or across the supply chain;
* identifying and allowing the sharing of best practice across projects within an organisation;
* using it to assess and present the findings from a variety of EVM reviews in a format that is easy to understand;
* facilitating comparisons with other projects;
* supporting the development of the business plan and strategy.

2.8.2 Assessment – the general process

There is no single, right way to perform the assessment using the maturity grid. The primary factors that determine the right approach for an organisation are its current culture and the desired outcomes from the assessment exercise. Different approaches deliver different benefits. Whichever approach is used, the key factor to remember is that assessment is about the continuous improvement of the project.

The greatest value from an assessment can be achieved if it involves someone who has a working knowledge of the implementation and operation of an EVM system. This ensures that the assessment can be completed with an understanding of the fine distinctions between the different maturity levels for each of the attributes that are scored.

The assessment can be performed in a number of different ways:

* self-assessment – from within the project;
* peer assessment – by other teams within the organisation;
* independent assessment – by reviewers external to the project.

The steps involved in the assessment are:

* form the team;
* assess the project against maturity levels;
* develop an action plan;
* reassess to measure improvement.

While the assessment is valuable, the most critical phase of the process is action planning and implementation. Having completed the diagnostic phase the following points should be considered:

* what identified strengths must be maintained to maximum effect?
* what identified strengths are to be developed and exploited even further?
* what areas for improvement are identified and critical to address?
* what areas for improvement have been identified but not pursued because they are not key to the business?
* how should progress be monitored against the agreed improvement actions?

The actions that are identified should be captured in a plan, with clearly defined responsibilities and timescales for their implementation. To help with the prioritisation of the actions a grid such as Figure 3 may be of benefit.

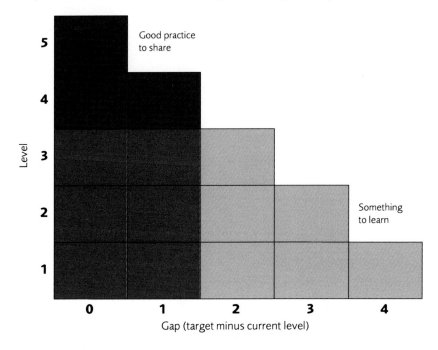

Figure 3: Action prioritisation
Taken from the *Earned Value Management Compass* (APM, 2010)

The grid can be used by taking the current score and identifying it on the vertical axis. Then taking the current score away from the target score identifies the position on the horizontal axis. The priority of the actions increases as the shade of blue darkens.

Where a project scores predominately light blue there is potential to share learning with other projects in the organisation that may also not be performing so well.

2.9 Defining an appropriate change plan to achieve the required target levels for a specific organisation

The results of the 'as is' analysis are registered in a change log along with the 'to be' target. A change plan is then produced and executed.

The change control process should include the following:

* **A change request:** a request with relevant information on the nature of the change. The change is entered into a change log, which is a register of all changes that have been requested whatever their status, for example, pending, approved, rejected or deferred;
* **Initial evaluation:** the change is reviewed to consider if it is worthwhile evaluating it in detail. The evaluation of change consumes resources, which in itself is a deviation from the project plan. The proposed change may be rejected without further evaluation;
* **Detailed evaluation:** the change is evaluated to consider the impact on the project's baseline scope, time, cost or quality objectives or agreed benefit.

Items to consider for a change plan include:
* tools;
* techniques;
* processes;
* behaviours;
* training/mentoring;
* stakeholder management plan;
* reporting process/project reviews;
* requirements to be satisfied;
* system design;
* Project Management Office (PMO) – central or team?
* people – internal and/or external resources;
* the business case;
* definition of finished end state;
* WBS creation;
* communications plan.

2.9.1 Considerations for a change plan:

Stage One
Appraise
Activities conducted at this stage could include:
* understanding the difference in the gap between now and the desired state;
* establishing what needs to change, what the desired end state needs to be and what will be the acceptance criteria for that end state. This will help to shape the scope of the business change project that needs to be delivered. This could include:
  * affordability and cost and the case for change;
  * shape of the organisation;
  * people capability in the organisation;
  * key capabilities required to deliver the solution – training, IT, etc.
  * engaging with key stakeholders;
  * identifying the key risks and enablers that can affect the successful delivery of the change project;
* undertaking a gap analysis to establish the potential size of the business change.

Stage Two
Design
This stage focuses on the detailed requirements to facilitate the solution, including:
* assessing the key capability requirements;
* developing an implementation plan;
* creating the necessary breakdown structures;
* creating the project processes that will ensure a robust long-term solution;
* developing and testing IT solutions and infrastructure;
* identifying skills development and creating training plans and material;
* looking at the design of the organisation including CAMs, support staff and management structure;
* identifying the number of roles required to support the activity;
* undertaking an initial stakeholder review of the impact of the proposed changes;
* identifying risks and potential mitigation plans;
* creating a communications plan to support the change.

Stage Three
Implementation
This stage focuses on the practical requirements of the solution, including:
- communication of the change;
- how the change affects people;
- the timescales involved;
- the requirements for CAMs, etc. to:
  - develop the local organisation models and resource requirements;
  - develop the breakdown structures, WBS/OBS/RAM;
  - develop modified statements of work (SoW);
  - attend training;
  - implement changes in toolsets, schedules, budgets, etc.;
  - maintain close support with the CAMs and teams throughout the transition;
  - test implementation using a self-assessment maturity model, for example, the *Earned Value Management Compass (APM, 2010)*;
  - test implementation using an independent verification, for example, IBR;
- conduct lessons learned.

2.10 Defining and implementing a project communications strategy and infrastructure

Communications strategy
A communications strategy documents how information will be disseminated to, and received from, all stakeholders in the activity (e.g. project or programme). It identifies the medium and frequency of communication between parties and it is used to establish and manage ongoing communications throughout a programme or project.

To successfully launch and maintain effective communication of an EVMS, it is essential that all personnel affected, both directly and indirectly, by the implementation are fully aware of the scope, scale and impact of the launch on the business. This needs to consider the following areas:
- stakeholder analysis highlighting key groups for communication;
- champions for communication;
- proposed communications mechanisms;
- communications material;
- feedback mechanisms.

Stakeholders
The following are the key stakeholder groups for communication activities:
Those driving change (champions for communication)
The main responsibilities for this group are to provide information about the progress being made on the launch and build commitment and confidence in the capability and benefits that are being delivered. It is also important to engage the organisation and solicit commitment for problem solving and enabling decision making.

Those defining or implementing change
This group focuses on the need to communicate specific information regarding process, IT and training development changes that are being implemented into the business. This should be done in a timely and appropriate manner to ensure smooth implementation and acceptance.

Those impacted by change
This group of stakeholders should be provided with the appropriate information and messages for the existing functions to enable them to understand how they can prepare and participate in the transition.

Those aware of change

This group should be kept informed of progress along with any issues relating to the EVM release.

Communication objectives

- To secure buy-in from key stakeholders and provide opportunities for them to show their support for the implementation programme.
- To create a 'pull' from the target population for the implementation of the EVM toolset and processes.
- To measure the customer population's current understanding of EVM and assess their specific needs.
- To implement a programme of regular 'no surprises' communications to meet the customer needs.
- To identify the key benefits and challenges (to the business and to the individual) of adopting EVM.
- To advertise the success of the launch.

Communication outcomes

The following outcomes are required following the communication process:

- all changes necessary for the effective implementation of the EVM toolset are accepted and understood;
- individuals have been identified and EVM roles and responsibilities agreed via the appropriate channels and IT toolsets, etc.;
- ongoing communications in place.

Key activities of the programme

The programme for the EVM launch should contain the following activities relating to communications:

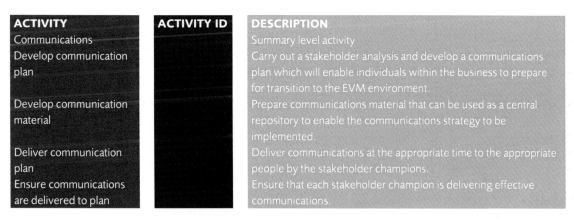

ACTIVITY	ACTIVITY ID	DESCRIPTION
Communications		Summary level activity
Develop communication plan		Carry out a stakeholder analysis and develop a communications plan which will enable individuals within the business to prepare for transition to the EVM environment.
Develop communication material		Prepare communications material that can be used as a central repository to enable the communications strategy to be implemented.
Deliver communication plan		Deliver communications at the appropriate time to the appropriate people by the stakeholder champions.
Ensure communications are delivered to plan		Ensure that each stakeholder champion is delivering effective communications.

Table 2: Communications plan development
Taken from the *Earned Value Management Compass* (APM, 2010)

Communication strategy

- Identify key stakeholders within the target population and their receptiveness to the launch.
- Involve key stakeholders in the development and implementation programme.
- Identify the key stakeholders as the vehicle for implementing the communication programme.
- Identify all personnel who will be affected by the implementation of the EVM environment.
- Build strong relationships with the key influencers and decision makers.
- Manage the customer/sponsor's expectations.
- Provide the opportunity for, and actively encourage, customer involvement in the development and implementation of EVM.
- Evaluate the customer's current understanding of EVM.
- Identify gaps in the customer's knowledge and understand their needs.
- Identify the most appropriate mechanism(s) for communicating to the customer.

- Encourage constructive feedback on all aspects of the release.
- Put the launch into context by communicating:
  - the EVM vision and programme;
  - the launch overview;
  - the launch detail;
  - what does it mean to the individual? (i.e. their role/job).
- Utilise existing communication channels within the organisation.
- Integrate the communication plan with the training plan.
- Define the method(s) of communication.

Communication materials

Standard briefing packs should be available for all levels of communication. This pack can then be tailored to the particular audience and should cover the following:

- overview:
  - the vision – why there is a need to change (current business environment/today's problems/issues/challenge of recent orders, building future business, customer requirements);
  - lessons learnt from previous organisational changes.
- EVM overview;
- project management processes;
- toolsets;
- roles and responsibilities;
- intranet and website;
- newsletters, team briefings, team boards and calendars.

Communications feedback mechanisms

In order to ensure that the communications plan is implemented effectively, the following reviews are proposed:

Progress reviews

The roll-out team will produce a monthly communications document to be distributed to the relevant champions for input to progress reviews. In order to do this, feedback is required on progress from the relevant champions.

Communication champion reviews

In addition to the progress reviews there needs to be a forum to review communications with all communication champions. This will specifically review:
- What was planned to be done?
- What communication has been done?
- Has it been effective? What needs to be done next if there are any variations?
- Delivery of the revised communications.

Review of individuals being communicated to

In order to build on the communication champion reviews, there should also be an assessment of the perceptions of the people being communicated to. This should either be undertaken by the roll-out team or by someone from an area with an independent view of the subject matter.
The options for this review will include:
- a questionnaire post-communication to specific groups;
- random phone calls/straw poll;
- face to face reviews;
- focus groups;
- team briefings.

Examples of the types of questions to ask include:
- What do you know about EVM – what is it going to deliver?
- Is the method of communication pertinent?
- Was the content of material pitched correctly?
- How often were you communicated to?
- Would you like more involvement with communications?
- Was the message clearly explained?
- Did you have the opportunity to ask questions?
- Were the questions answered honestly/clearly?

Fitness for purpose checklist
Has the information given to stakeholders met their requirements?
Has the information received from stakeholders met the programme/project owner's requirements?
Has all the necessary information been disseminated?
Have the roles and responsibilities of the individuals involved in the communication strategy been understood by them?
Have these roles been carried out satisfactorily?

Table 3: Fitness for purpose checklist

Notes:
Suggested content of a communication strategy:
- a list of stakeholders and their information requirements;
- communication mechanisms to be used (for example, written reports, seminars, workshops, videos, emails, newsletters);
- the key elements of information to be distributed by the different mechanisms – including frequency and information collection and collation;
- the roles and responsibilities of key individuals responsible for ensuring communication is adequate/appropriate and timely;
- the identification of how unexpected/unscheduled information from other parties (including stakeholders) will be handled within the scope of the activity.

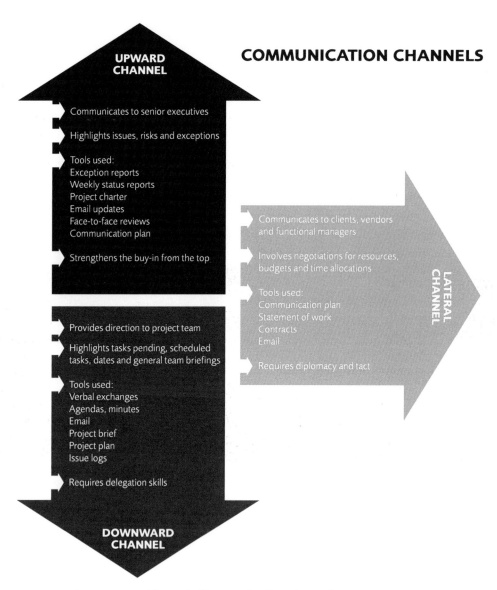

COMMUNICATION CHANNELS

UPWARD CHANNEL

Communicates to senior executives

Highlights issues, risks and exceptions

Tools used:
Exception reports
Weekly status reports
Project charter
Email updates
Face-to-face reviews
Communication plan

Strengthens the buy-in from the top

Provides direction to project team

Highlights tasks pending, scheduled
tasks, dates and general team briefings

Tools used:
Verbal exchanges
Agendas, minutes
Email
Project brief
Project plan
Issue logs

Requires delegation skills

DOWNWARD CHANNEL

Communicates to clients, vendors
and functional managers

Involves negotiations for resources,
budgets and time allocations

Tools used:
Communication plan
Statement of work
Contracts
Email

Requires diplomacy and tact

LATERAL CHANNEL

Figure 4: Communication channels
(Reproduced with kind permission from BMTHiQSigma)

The communications plan

The following information should be contained within the project communications plan:

- the project communication strategy;
- details of, and information from, the kick-off meeting;
- the roles and responsibilities of the team;
- details of project status meetings and frequency;
- change control communications;
- details of project review meetings;
- information on the transition from deployment to operations;
- details of the closure meeting.

An effective communications plan will:

facilitate team development: proper communication provides the basis for the project team to work together and understand the objectives and tasks to be completed. Better communication ultimately means better performance;

be used throughout the process: from defining the user requirements to implementing the product, a proper communication plan informs all project stakeholders which communication channels will be used on the project, who will report to whom, and the frequency, type, and format of project meetings;

make it easier to update stakeholders: frequent communications keep stakeholders in the loop and can facilitate acceptance of the project;

prevent ad hoc additional project documentation: taking effective communication steps from the day the project starts will result in less ad hoc project documentation. Ad hoc documentation is not routinely circulated to everyone and can create confusion amongst the project participants.

Communication aids	
Type/technique	**Description**
Email	Allows project teams to communicate text, audio and video files between team members.
Interoffice memos	Provide a formal forum to communicate key dates, policies and procedures.
Instant messaging (IM)	Allows team members to communicate real-time.
Project status meetings	Provide regular status updates and reviews of the project.
Telephone/video conferences	Provide a medium to involve team members located in other geographic regions
Intranet, internet boards	Formally communicate status, progress, highlights and objectives to all.
Project road shows	Provide feedback to stakeholders or users.
Walkabouts	Involve a hands-on face-to-face, approach with the team and clients.

Table 4: Recommended types of communication aid
(Reproduced with kind permission from BMTHiQSigma)

3 Definition

3.1 The definition of Statement of Work (SoW)

A SoW defines the scope of a project, including the overall requirements and deliverables for that project. It forms the basis for allocating work, budget and schedule requirements.

The extent to which the SoW fully describes the requirements of the project will have a direct impact on the ability of the EVMS to provide objective measures of performance against the original project requirement.

3.2 The definition, diagram and purpose of an organisation breakdown structure

Projects usually involve people from a variety of functions and departments across an organisation. A fundamental requirement of a well-managed project is clear people organisation. Where matrix management structures are used, this clarity in organisational definition is particularly important.

In order to clarify and define the organisation, an organisation chart or organisation breakdown structure (OBS) should be developed. Roles, responsibilities and accountabilities should be clearly defined for all staff and communicated across the project team. Staff being introduced into the project should have a clear knowledge of whom they report to, and for what work they are responsible.

Vague definitions of roles, responsibilities, authorities and accountabilities will lead to ambiguities and confusion in the management of the project.

3.3 The definition and structure of a Work Breakdown Structure (WBS)

The hierarchical sub-division of a project into discrete elements of work is known as a work breakdown structure (WBS). The WBS is developed by identifying high-level elements of work necessary to meet the project requirements. These major elements are then broken down into smaller components. This breakdown continues until the lowest level of detail deemed necessary for management visibility and control is established. All aspects of the contract are included and the WBS can be viewed as a graphical, hierarchical representation of the SoW.

When developing a WBS, it is advisable to concentrate solely on the work content of the project. Projects may use a work breakdown structure dictionary (WBSD), the purpose of which is to describe the entire scope of work to be undertaken within the project. It must capture the contract scope and all contract requirements. To enable this to be checked it must provide a ready reference between the WBS and contract elements. It also provides the basis for the SoW included on the control account plans.

For each element of the WBS, the dictionary should contain:

* a contract number;
* a WBS number and title;
* the WBSD issue number and date;
* the contract paragraph number;
* a SoW including all contract deliverables to be produced as part of the work element.

The WBS dictionary should include all elements to be sub-contracted and should specifically identify the sub-contractor undertaking the WBS element.

3.4 The definition and purpose of a control account

A WBS reflects the way in which work has been sub-divided. To assign work responsibilities to appropriate organisational elements the WBS must be interrelated with the OBS. The assignment of lower-level work breakdown elements to responsible organisations provides a key control point for management purposes and for cost collection.

The integration of the WBS and the OBS at the control account level can be displayed as a matrix, with the OBS elements listed on one axis and the WBS elements on the other. This is the responsibility assignment matrix (RAM), where each element is a control account (CA), with a control account manager (CAM) responsible for its completion to budget.

A CA will normally comprise a number of WPs, although in some cases a control account may be a single work package. Each work package should have the following attributes:

* a defined scope of work;
* information on measure of achievement;
* traceability up through the WBS;
* a budget;
* details of assignment of responsibility;
* start and finish dates.

If it is not possible to define a work package to the detail mentioned above, then it should be identified as a planning package within the CA.

3.4.1 Process discussion

Once the work breakdown structure (WBS), and the dictionary, if used, have been completed, they should be reconciled back to the requirement, along with any other formal agreements, to ensure that all aspects of the project have been included.

It is important that the CA is identified for each work area. The CA is the main action point for the planning and control of project work. It is the point where management responsibility for the individual CAs is assigned. A manager may be responsible for many CAs, but a CA should have only one manager.

The CA in an integrated management system is the lowest level in the structure at which comparisons between actual costs and budgeted costs are normally required by management. However, analysis will also be done at lower levels, as required for local control. Most management actions taken at higher levels are triggered by significant problems identified at the CA level. For this reason, the levels selected for the establishment of the organisation and the CAs should be carefully considered at the outset of the project.

3.5 The definition and purpose of a responsibility assignment matrix

A responsibility assignment matrix (RAM) is a diagram or chart showing assigned responsibilities for elements of the project's work. It is created by combining the WBS with the organisation breakdown structure (OBS).

The RAM shows the level of control that has been established. If the accounts identified are too big or too small, too many or too few, they should be reconsidered and changed accordingly.

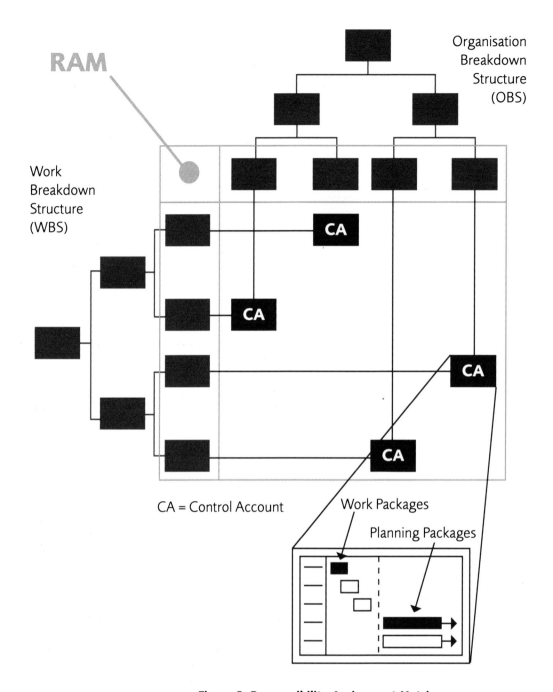

RAM

Organisation
Breakdown
Structure
(OBS)

Work
Breakdown
Structure
(WBS)

CA

CA

CA

CA

CA = Control Account

Work Packages

Planning Packages

Figure 5: Responsibility Assignment Matrix
Taken from the *Earned Value Management: APM Guidelines* (2008)

3.6 The factors influencing the appropriate details in a statement of work

The statement of work (SoW) should be derived from the project scope statement during the project planning phase, in which the project outputs are detailed. The objective of the SoW is to describe the work expected with as much clarity and detail as possible in order to produce the project deliverables.

The SoW may be used by the project manager as a governance tool to ensure that all project deliverables are documented, and should be written before work is planned or scheduled in detail. A SoW should be developed for all elements of a project WBS.

The language used in a SoW should be clear and specific to describe what needs to be done (for example, use verbs and include quantities and numbers). Avoid vague terms that do not clearly support measurable deliverables, for example:

• research;
• develop;
• support;
• consider;
• mature.

A SoW must clearly identify what the work is and what it involves, for example, literature reviewing, design modelling, testing, analysis and report preparation. Be clear about the required outputs from test or analysis activities.

A SoW should be considered a mandatory project deliverable, irrespective of whether the work is being delivered by internal resources or by external vendors or contractors. It is considered good practice to clearly define both internally and externally contracted work.

The SoW forms the basis of each procurement activity, and its contents should be reflected in the procurement documents, for example a request for proposal or a request for quotation, and in the final contract award document. It should not attempt to duplicate or contradict terms and conditions contained elsewhere in the contract documents.

The more comprehensive the SoW is, the smaller the risk of scope change or scope creep. The contract schedule and PMB should be developed from the SoW. The SoW may be supplemented with additional technical reference documents and attachments. It is worth noting that any errors or omissions in the SoW, that are included in the contract, will inevitably lead to a contract change request and an amendment to the PMB.

Although no formal legal contracts are used for internal project deliverables, the SoW methodology should still be applied to ensure the same attention and precision is applied and that internal resourcing can be planned to meet the deliverables.

The factors influencing the appropriate level of detail of the SoW are outlined in the following 15 SoW components. These are intended to guide project managers to capture all the relevant information. The scope of work, period of performance and deliverables schedule are all mandatory information and the additional contents should be applied when appropriate.

1. Scope

The scope of a project consists of a detailed description of the work, the project background, the software and hardware to be used, and the exact nature of the work. The SoW should start with the high level deliverables (the what, when and where) of the scope statement and then break this detail down further into tangible, measurable products. It is important to identify what must be delivered and by whom.

2. Costs

Anticipated costs or estimates may be outlined for internal and cost-reimbursable type contracts, but are generally not included for firm fixed-price contracts.

3. Period of performance

This is the start and finish date for the project, along with the maximum billable hours per time period.

4. Deliverables

The SoW should list significant deliverables that represent the major output milestones, or deliverables that could have an impact on the critical path. Lower level tactical deliverables should be identified through the project schedule.

5. Deliverables schedule

This details the due dates for the project deliverables and includes such information as completion dates for development, QA testing and user acceptance testing.

6. Project governance

This describes the project governance structure, decision making authority, frequency of engagement and escalation procedures.

7. Project control procedures

These procedures detail the means of controlling the work, how performance will be measured and how payment criteria will be assessed and made in line with performance and deliverables.

8. Reporting requirements

Reporting requirements describe the type, data content, format and frequency of any performance or status reports required for the duration of the contract. They also include mandatory meeting attendance and any participation expected in project governance reviews, for example:

- weekly status reports;
- weekly meetings;
- monthly progress reports;
- project management team (PMT) meetings;
- programme reviews;
- outlines and drafts.

9. Assumptions

SoWs should only list significant, local assumptions. There is no need to list universal project assumptions which have been documented elsewhere. Assumptions are things that are believed to be true. This may include assumptions related to technical, resource and budget information. Assumptions should always be explicit and clearly stated.

10. Exclusions

SoWs should only list significant local exclusions. Exclusions should explicitly state what is not included in the project; this may include exclusions related to technical, resource and budget information. There is no need to list project exclusions which have been documented elsewhere. Exclusions should always be explicit and clearly stated.

11. Risks

Where there is a down-side in the event of an assumption not being true, this should be identified as a risk. Where risks are included in the SoW, they should be stated using a standard form of:

"There is a risk that <....> as a result of <...> with the impact that <....>".

However, all significant risks to the overall project should already have been included in the risk log.

12. Location

Locations should be specified where places of work other than a standard location are involved. This would be applicable to a SoW where work is to be performed either offsite or offshore.

13. Applicable standards

Industry standards or other standards to be imposed on the project deliverables should be highlighted. These include any standards, for example ISO, BSI.

14. Acceptance criteria

Quality standards that must be met, for example zero priority 1 defects, should be specified. Ensure any other conditions that must be met, such as number of test cases, number of test cases executed etc., are clarified.

15. Specialised requirements

Information including any special qualifications for the workforce, such as APMP Certified Project Manager, travel requirements and co-location requirements that are not covered by other contract details should all be detailed.

3.7 The purpose and approach for communicating the work breakdown structure amongst the project team and stakeholders

It is important to ensure all stakeholders have a consistent view of the project scope to ensure everyone has the same expectations and understanding of processes and deliverables.

The project manager should obtain acceptance and approval of the SoW from the project sponsor and/or the project customer. This represents the official scope baseline and expected final products.

The SoW can now be used to communicate the scope baseline to the project team, who will use the statement to develop the WBS in further detail. All elements described in the statement should be reflected in the WBS along with the identified start and finish dates and/or durations. This enables the project schedule and activities to be developed with durations and dependencies included. The resultant milestone deliverables' dates in the completed schedule should be validated against the dates set out in the baseline requirements.

The SoW, WBS and baseline schedule together enable clear and accurate communications to project stakeholders, describing what needs to be done and by when. It is the starting point for assigning ownership of the work and resource loading the schedule, and it enables the internal and external procurement activities to begin.

Any subsequent approved scope changes should be updated in the SoW, WBS and baseline schedule.

3.8 The skills and abilities needed by control account managers

The definition of a control account manager (CAM) is 'the performing manager who is responsible for planning, performing and monitoring the elements of work defined within that control account' (*Value Management APM Guidelines*, 2008).

3.8.1 Duties and responsibilities
The skills and abilities required by a CAM need to be defined along with the role's responsibilities at the various stages of the project lifecycle. Overall, CAMs are responsible for the management of CAs and accountable for the delivery of CA outputs within an agreed schedule and budget targets within the project lifecycle. Where appropriate, CAMs are also responsible for managing contracts and the contract deliverables.

During the **definition** phase of a project, the CAM has specific responsibility for:

1. the definition of the SoW and associated WBS dictionary elements, ensuring the SoW is fully captured;
2. planning and scheduling;
3. time-phasing of budget assignments (labour and non-labour);
4. the selection of appropriate EVTs;
5. control account monitoring;
6. variance justification and exception reporting;
7. CA status management;
8. the identification of appropriate changes to maintain baseline integrity.

Each CAM will separate their WBS tasks hierarchically into discrete areas of work. Appropriate schedule measurement milestones, including key events such as design reviews, governance and maturity gates, and deliverables such as drawing completion and sub-assembly completion, will be identified. These outputs should also be identified as a basis of physical accomplishment.

Key responsibilities at this stage are:

- reviewing the risk register for risk identification and analysis;
- preparing the WBS dictionary entry/entries for the allocated CAs;
- cross referencing the work scope to the risk register and contractual SoW;
- agreeing and accepting major assumptions;
- agreeing and accepting major milestones.

In the **planning** phase of a project the key responsibilities of a CAM are:

- producing detailed schedules;
- identifying and defining WPs and PPs;
- negotiating/agreeing cross CA dependencies (horizontal integration);
- defining the resources required to discharge the scope of the CA. These must be defined in terms of resource types (for example, direct labour, equipment, materials, etc.).

During this planning phase CAMs also have responsibility for budgeting and work authorisation aspects of their part of a project. These include:

- negotiating and agreeing the CA budget;
- selecting and assigning an EVT for each work package;
- agreeing the CA plan, including major bought out and sub-contract items, with the project manager;
- reviewing and accepting/rejecting CA work authorisation document;
- confirming the material and sub-contract requirements and associated EVTs.

During the **data collection** and **analysis, review and action** phase of a project, the CAM is responsible for:

- verifying accuracy of the EV data;
- correcting data issues, as appropriate;
- raising ACWP transfers where appropriate for incorrect bookings;
- updating schedule progress at appropriate intervals;
- identifying and logging management actions;
- creating a CA level progressed schedule and critical paths specific to their CA, as appropriate;
- analysing their CA level schedules, identifying and implementing any required actions;
- analysing work package listing/requirements checks;
- evaluating estimate to completion (ETC) data to determine estimate at completion (EAC). Re-evaluate the EAC where a significant change is detected;
- performing variance analysis on threshold breaches;
- identifying any appropriate corrective actions;
- escalating any issues as appropriate;
- ensuring corrective actions are implemented;
- converting PPs into detailed WPs as appropriate.

During this ongoing phase the CAM's duties on a daily, weekly and monthly basis will include reviewing the existing activities, along with the activities that are due to start. The CAM will need to check that progress is on schedule and to budget, and that the required reports are completed. The table below details the CAM's responsibilities on a daily, weekly and monthly basis.

Frequency	Task
Daily	Enter, validate and update task and activity progress; check and enter any tasks that are due to start or finish.
Weekly	Review activities that are due to start in the next week, ensure that all actions are in place to enable this to happen.
	Review activities that are due to finish in the next week, make sure that these are progressing to plan.
	Review activities that are running behind (or ahead of) schedule and ensure necessary actions are taken to minimise effect on the overall programme.
	Review activities which are running over/under budget, establish reasons for the underspend/overspend and ensure that the effects of this are kept to a minimum.
Monthly	Each month the same reviews that have been conducted on a weekly basis need to be repeated, but with emphasis on the month ahead.
	Produce monthly reports narrative and an estimate to completion (ETC) as per the reporting cycle schedule.
	Review the horizontal (other cost account) and vertical dependencies.

Table 5: CAM tasks with recommended review frequency

The CAM's responsibilities for revisions, data maintenance and change management as part of a project's change management process are:

- to identify and raise change requests;
- to provide supporting rationale and data for change requests;
- to approve changes to the baseline within constraints and beyond the rolling wave horizon;
- to assist project coordination with the embodiment of changes;
- to ensure all approved changes to the PMB are implemented within the required timescales in accordance with change control procedures;
- to convert PPs to WPs using appropriate documents.

3.8.2 Control account manager skills and abilities

From the information mentioned above it is clear that a CAM needs to have knowledge and experience of:

- planning;
- scheduling;
- change management;
- risk management;
- variance analysis;
- data collection;
- resource allocation;
- EVM and EVTs;
- soft skills;
- report production;
- resource management;
- budgeting, cost and financial management.

CAMs need to be able to efficiently and effectively manage the work area(s) allocated to them and be capable of motivating and encouraging their project team. They should also possess the knowledge in the technical or operational area relevant to the project and their CA.

CAMs should be effective team leaders (in terms of teamwork, communication and planning), and experienced in project management, with strong people management skills.

3.9 The processes necessary for managing a control account

CAMs will need to be familiar with a number of processes to effectively and efficiently manage a CA. These include, but are not limited to, the following processes:

- definition;
- planning;
- scheduling;
- data collection;
- monitoring;
- analysis;
- change management;
- risk management;
- work authorisation;
- budgeting, cost and financial management.

The following matrix indicates the processes used in the various phases of managing a project.

	Definition (organisation)	Planning (planning and scheduling)	Planning (budgeting and work authorisation)	Analysis, review and action (analysis and management reporting)	Change management (revisions, data maintenance and change management)
Definition	x				
Planning	X	X			
Scheduling		x			
Work authorisation			x		
Budgeting			x		
Data collection				x	
Monitoring				x	
Analysis				x	
Change management					x
Risk management	X	X	X	X	X

Table 6: Processes necessary for managing a control account

The process is also well illustrated in this flow chart:

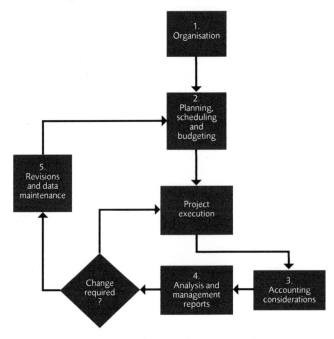

Figure 6: Process of managing a control account

Reproduced by kind permission from the Planning, Monitoring and Control SIG

3.10 Principles for the correct design of a responsibility assignment matrix

Principles for the design of a responsibility assignment matrix (RAM) that should be considered include:

- a CA is allocated to one CAM;
- all CAs must be mapped to a CAM;
- traceability – the amount in the CA plan should equal the CA amount in the RAM;
- the sum of work scope – all CAs should equal the PMB value;
- the RAM could be at different levels or layers. Consider tolerances for each CA in terms of control and reporting purposes;
- identify who is responsible for the delivery of products and/or work within a CA;
- a CA where the CAM has no responsibility for budget control.

3.11 The requirements for integrating sub-contract management into an earned value system

It is appropriate to reflect the requirements of *Earned Value Management: APM Guidelines* (APM, 2008) in any sub-contract. Reporting requirements should be consistent with the project size, risk, complexity and other factors.

Processes should be in place to ensure that the sub-contractor's plans are represented within the project plans/schedules in order to derive a view of total project performance. Project plans can be very large and complex and decisions should be taken regarding the level of detail to be incorporated into the plans. If there is too much detail, the maintenance of the plan becomes a burdensome overhead, while if there is insufficient detail, the exact status of the project is difficult to ascertain.

The supplier's plans should detail the appropriate number of activities/milestones required to effectively track and manage progress. These activities will be shown in the project schedule as either WPs/PPs or as individual CAs, depending on the level of detail to be reported. Whatever the level of incorporation, sufficient detail to provide visibility of the actual status and early warning of potential problems and issues is vital. It is also important to structure the CAs/WPs to enable the recording of both in-house supplier management and specific sub-contractor efforts.

The resourcing/budgeting of the work should reflect the value of the item or service – as agreed in the contract – to allow a realistic expenditure profile or budget curve to be generated. Furthermore, there should be a discrete milestone identified in every reporting period to allow the measurement of achievement on a regular basis. However, the supplier should be expected to provide a monthly progress report (or equivalent), irrespective of the detail of their schedule contained within the project schedule. This report can be used as the basis for claiming achievement (or otherwise).

The way in which sub-contractor effort is integrated into the baseline (Figure 7) will differ according to their importance to the project. The distinction between major and minor sub-contractors should be based upon factors such as equipment value, criticality (risk) to the project (e.g. single source supply) and/or whether they are an off-the-shelf supplier. Ideally, major sub-contractors should be structured as single CAs, not only because of their relative importance but also to provide the ability to clearly monitor their overall status.

Minor sub-contractors should be structured within single WPs/PPs, with a CA conceivably containing several minor sub-contractors. This still allows for appropriate visibility of performance, but not at the lower levels within the integrated baseline.

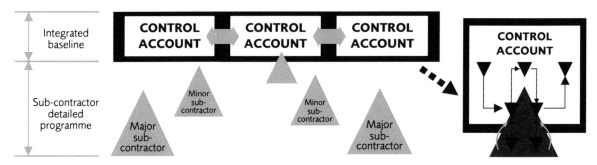

Figure 7: Integration of sub-contract effort

Taken from the *Earned Value Management: APM Guidelines* (2008)

3.12 The need to flow down the earned value system requirements to sub-contractors appropriately, based on size, complexity and type of contract

Contractual requirement

The customer may have specified that sub-contractors with a work package over a certain value have to comply with the EV system requirements placed on the prime contractor.

Company standard approach

The organisation may specify that EV system requirements apply throughout the supply chain above a certain value or with a given level of risk.

Sub-contractors and progress measurement

Where a significant element of the project is sourced with sub-contractors and the level of progress measurement through the standard payment milestones/stage payments is not sufficient to provide the necessary level of confidence.

Considerations

*   Increased sub-contract cost. The sub-contractor may respond that the additional reporting burden will incur an additional cost.
*   Increased levels of data to be analysed and incorporated with the project progress data.
*   Increased data integrity analysis. Can the externally provided EV data be automatically incorporated within the project data or will it require cleansing or filtering?
*   Increased requirement for process, system and data review. Who will be responsible for ensuring compliance with the requirements? Will the customer include the sub-contractors in their integrated baseline reviews, compliance reviews, readiness reviews, etc. or will the prime contractor be given this burden?
*   If the data is wrong, who is responsible? The sub-contractor or prime contractor?
*   How will the change management process ensure that the flow down of contractual change or other baseline change does not adversely impact the schedule?
*   To what level should the requirement be flowed down within the sub-contractor's work package?
*   How does the sub-contractor measure progress?
*   Does the supplier already have a compliant EVM process in place? Do they already report EVM to other customers? If so, there should be little additional burden on the sub-contractor. If not, what does the sub-contractor need to do?
*   Can progress measurement be linked to payment milestones that are physical deliverables?

3.13 The need to flow down the scope of work to a control account and ensure commitment and authorisation

To ensure that all work is formally managed through to delivery it must be allocated down to at least CA level as indicated in figure 8 below. Without the allocation to a CAM, no formal responsibility and accountability for delivery is established within the system.

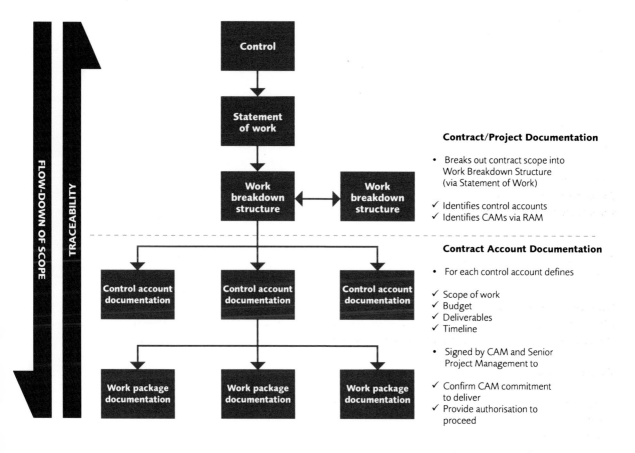

Figure 8: Control account flow-down scope
Reproduced with kind permission from BMTHiQSigma

The SoW, delivery timeframe and associated budget for each CA is documented and signed by both the CAM and appropriate representatives of the senior project management team. This achieves two main aims:

1. **commitment**
   It provides confirmation from the CAM that the documented scope, budget and timescale form a realistic and achievable work package that they can commit to deliver;

2. **authorisation**
   It enables the senior project management team to provide the CAM with the authorisation to deliver the SoW within the agreed constraints.

3.14 Judging the level of risk, uncertainty, complexity and novelty in a given statement of work

Projects are unique, transient activities undertaken to achieve a desired outcome. This suggests that all projects are therefore different, and that different management approaches and plans will be required for every project. Projects can therefore fall into different categories. It is useful in the early planning stage to decide what type a project is. One example of categorisation is:

* **runner** (something we know how to do, easy to plan and estimate, which is low risk and easy to execute);
* **repeater** (a runner with a difference, something outside the norm);
* **stranger** (something we have little experience of but know can be done, harder to plan and estimate, with a higher risk, and harder to execute);
* **alien** (a project nobody has done before, hard to plan and estimate, with a high risk and is as yet unclear how to execute).

When estimating and planning, the above categorisation will drive the approach taken, and the levels of accuracy and precision that can be expected. This approach is particularly useful when assessing a SoW for the aspects detailed below.

Risk
An uncertain event or set of events that, should they occur, will have an effect on the achievement of the objectives.

Uncertainty
Uncertainty is the lack of complete certainty, the existence of more than one possibility. The true outcome, state, result or value is not yet known.

Complexity
Complexity describes activities and/or tasks are characterised by the fact that:

* are characterised by uncertainty, ambiguity, dynamic interfaces and significant political or external influences;
* may run over a period of time which exceeds the technology cycle time of the technologies involved;
* the results can be defined by either outcomes and/or benefits but not by outputs.

The following categories may be used to help understand project and product complexity:

* **Assembly project or product:** this is based on a sub-system, component or assembly.
  Examples include the design of a single service or the design and development of sticky notes.

* **System project or product:** this can be either a system or a platform of systems.
  Examples include developing a new computer, a single building construction or a production plant redevelopment.

* **Array project or product:** this may be a system of systems or an array of products.
  Examples include a new neighbourhood building construction, an underground railway tunnel or a nationwide mobile telephone network.

Novelty
Novelty relates to how new the end product is (or will be) to its customers and users. The degree of novelty can be expressed as categories; for example, derivative, platform and breakthrough.

Derivative: either extending or improving existing products and/or services.
Examples include developing a new edition of an existing car, upgrading an existing production facility or streamlining quality procedures and/or processes.

Platform: developing and producing new types of products and/or services for existing markets, customers and clients. Examples include developing a new type of car or developing a new type of helicopter.

Breakthrough: Introducing a new concept, a new idea or a new use of a product that the market, customers and clients would not have seen before.
Examples include the first all-electric car, the first unmanned aircraft, the first tilt-rotor aircraft, the first mobile telephone or the compact disc (CD).

Technology

The level of technological uncertainty can affect project delivery timescales and costs. The level of technological uncertainty can be divided into four levels:

- low-tech;
- medium-tech;
- high-tech;
- super high-tech.

Level of technological uncertainty				
	Low-tech	**Medium-tech**	**High-tech**	**Super high-tech**
Definitions	Uses only existing, well established and mature technologies.	Mostly existing technologies; limited technology or a new feature.	Uses many new, recently developed, existing technologies.	Key project technologies do not exist at time of project initiation.
Examples	Road building, build-to-print.	Derivatives or improvements of products or new models in established industries (e.g. domestic appliances).	New systems in fast-moving industries (e.g. computers, telecommunications).	New, unproven concepts beyond the technological state of the art (e.g. Mars space mission).

Table 7: Level of technological uncertainty

Pace (or speed)

The pace or speed at which a project needs to be delivered is also an important factor. The following table details levels of pace that may be used to understand the type of project being undertaken.

	Regular	Fast/competitive	Time-critical	Blitz
Definitions	Time not critical to organisational success.	Completion on time is important for company's competitive advantage.	Meeting the time goal is critical for project success. Any delay would mean project failure.	Crisis projects; urgent; project must be completed as soon as possible.
Examples	Government initiatives, public works.	Business-related projects; new product introduction; new plant construction in response to increased market demand.	Projects with a definite deadline or window of opportunity; space launch restricted by time window; Y2K project.	War; response to natural disasters; rapid response to business-related surprises or incidents.

Table 8: Level of pace or speed in a project

3.15 Defining clear deliverables that meet stakeholders' requirements

A deliverable can be defined as any measurable, tangible, verifiable item that must be produced to complete the project. It is a term often used more narrowly in reference to an external deliverable that is subject to approval by the project sponsor or customer.

It is not always easy to clearly define deliverables. If the project is to create a product, then the deliverables may be tangible. However, some projects are more speculative, for example, research where the deliverable may be less defined and will include reports, test results, risk assessments and documentation. In these cases a more subjective approach is required to progress the project because management decisions regarding the continuation of funding and project progression are less securely established.

3.16 Developing a work breakdown structure for a specific project and organisation

A work breakdown structure (WBS) breaks the project down hierarchically into meaningful work packages to a point of single accountability. It covers the full scope where the lowest level WBS elements have unique work content. It will also influence the way in which the project incurs actual costs, reports progress and measures achievement.

An overarching factor in establishing a WBS is the complexity of the project. There are various factors for establishing a project's complexity, for example:

* the stability of the project – product novelty, requirements stability, uncertainty of methods;
* political, economic, sociological, technical (PEST), legal and environmental implications;
* financial impacts;
* stakeholder alignment;
* strategic importance to the organisation;
* interfaces with other organisations.

All these factors will influence the depth of the WBS decomposition and its breadth.

Having identified the project's complexity, the appropriateness of the WBS should be assessed and the required depth of WBS decomposition should be understood. Stopping the WBS at too high a level will have both disadvantages and advantages.

Advantages	Disadvantages
Fewer people are involved in the project decision-making process.	Increases the workload for a single person to plan the work and manage its execution.
Relationships between work packages in all parts of the WBS may be communicated better.	The owner of the work may be tempted to plan at a higher level of detail than may be required, which will lead to the incorrect granularity of planning. This may not be good enough to establish the true critical path and result in risks and opportunities within the plan not being identified.

Creating a WBS that breaks the work down to too low a level will also have its disadvantages and advantages.

Advantages	Disadvantages
Obtains a detailed understanding of relationships and risks.	May plan at too low a detail, creating an increased workload to collect actual costs, report progress and measure achievement.
Understanding the breakdown of variances at a WBS level may be easier.	Creates a critical path at too low a level to manage the work efficiently and effectively.
During execution, any deviations from the plan are seen and understood earlier.	Increased relationships with other work packages may become burdensome.

This can be achieved by:

- cross-referencing the WBS with the SoW. This will better ensure that insignificant work is not planned, and will establish uniqueness for a WBS element's work content;
- using a verb when naming a WBS element. This will better ensure the WBS captures the work, and not just a product, organisation or cost. Good examples include 'create test procedures' and 'supply tooling'.

A WBS is a live document which is key to understanding, reporting and communicating a project's current state and progress made within it. Therefore it must be version controlled and dated so that all stakeholders are using the same up-to-date WBS, which should be stored in an accessible location.

Common mistakes when creating a WBS may be as follows:

- it is based on a product or organisation;
- it is too detailed or lacks detail;
- it does not contain the entire scope of the project;
- not all elements are mapped to the SoW;
- there is more than one owner at the CA level;
- it is not documented, visible to relevant stakeholders or version controlled.

4 Planning

4.1 What is a work package?

The work package is the lowest level at which performance data is normally analysed. It is therefore important to balance the length and scope of the work package against reporting cycle lengths, and to consider when and how to earn 'value'. Each work package must have a clearly defined start condition and finish point, with all deliverables defined. The scope of each work package must be unambiguously defined with the procedures to be followed identified. Each work package comprises a number of activities to be performed.

See section 4.22 on page 71 for more information on the types of work packages.

4.2 What is a planning package?

Planning packages (PPs) represent work that cannot yet be planned as work packages because of a lack of detailed information. Normally this is future work that is not scheduled to be started for at least three full months from the current date. Work in the near future that cannot be planned in work packages may indicate a problem of work definition.

PPs are structured below the control account level, have a defined scope of work and are allocated a time-phased budget. They have scheduled start and finish dates (hence a duration) and a defined budget and scope.

Planning packages must be converted into work packages before work can commence upon them, i.e. before they can 'earn' achievement, or have costs booked against them. The budget is withdrawn from the planning package and is used to establish work packages as their start date nears and the details of the tasks become clearer. The resulting work packages will contain the detailed activities, logic, milestones, resources and achievement measures.

4.3 What is an activity?

Each work package comprises a number of activities to be performed. Each activity can be assigned to only a single work package. Each activity is a stepping stone towards completion of its parent work package. Figure 9 shows a schematic of the relationship between work packages, planning packages and activities. The activity is where duration, resources and costs are estimated; dependencies are shown between activities.

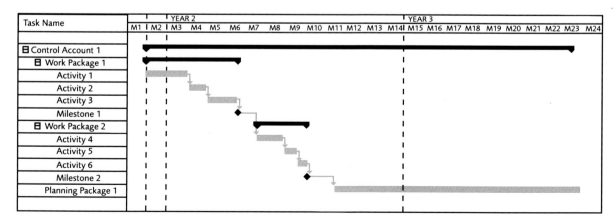

Figure 9: The relationship between control account, work package and activity
Taken from the *Earned Value Management: APM Guidelines* (2008)

4.4 The definition of rolling wave planning

The requirement for a periodic conversion, from planning package to work package, is the result of setting up the project using rolling wave planning, whereby only the current phase of a project is planned in detail and future phases are planned in outline. The conversion process is a fundamental aspect of project control using EVM and results in a more controlled project baseline.

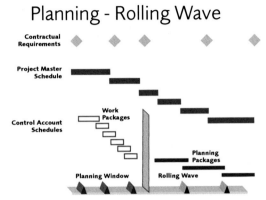

Figure 10: An illustration of rolling wave planning
Reproduced with kind permission from BAE SYSTEMS

4.5 What is a schedule?

Scheduling is the process of determining when project activities will take place, depending on defined durations and preceding activities. Schedule logic specifies when an activity should start or end on the basis of duration, predecessors, external predecessor relationships, resource availability or target dates.

Schedules can be created to reflect various elements of the WBS, from the highest-level plan to detailed work package schedules containing the lowest level of activity. These schedules form the basis for assessing actual progress and comparing actual cost against work performed.

All contractual milestones should be included within the schedule from the start of the project. These contractual milestones should be logically linked to appropriate activities so that any changes to forecast dates are applied throughout the schedule.

It is essential in any EVMS that activities on the current critical path are identified. This will enable variances from the plan to be appropriately categorised – e.g. 'late but float remains' as opposed to 'late and on critical path'. To preclude excessive workload on large projects, a project may choose to exclude the lower levels of schedules from the network used for critical path analyses. However, the lower-level schedules must always support the summary-level schedule so that all analyses have the same basis.

The overall scheduling process permits the integrated planning of project resources with the cost and schedule objectives of the project, and provides a means of measuring progress against planned effort. Scheduling and work scope definitions are prerequisites for basic project management and effective cost control.

4.6 Setting budgets

Budgeting is the process of distributing or allocating cost targets to individual segments of work. Strict budget element relationships must exist at all times in order to ensure that the sum of the parts is equal to the whole. The hierarchy of budget elements is shown in Figure 11. This illustrates how the intermediate summations are defined leading to the contract budget baseline.

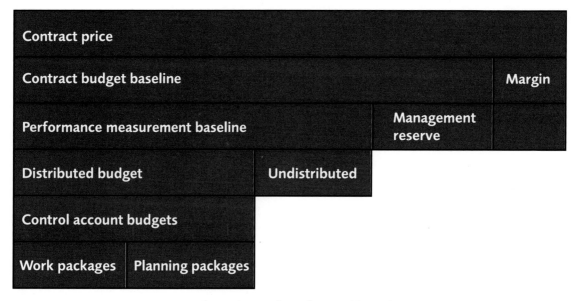

Figure 11: Budget element hierarchy
Taken from the *Earned Value Management: APM Guidelines* (2008)

4.7 The difference between budgets and funds

Within an EVM system the concept of budgets is different from the concept of funds. While a budget represents the cost performance target for a specific effort, funds represent the money available for expenditure in the accomplishment of the effort. Budgets are established for the relevant elements of the work breakdown structure and are time-phased.

Budget cannot be spent; it is the funds that are consumed. Funds are authorised by the customer or by the company on a total or periodic basis.

The formulation of estimates at completion (EACs) provides the project with visibility of the anticipated/out turn funds required by forecasting the actual funding requirements for any approved statement of work element.

4.8 The definition of cost types and rates that may be used

Projects usually involve many different types of costs that need to be summarised through various levels of detail. As work packages are subdivisions of work, then each work package will comprise a number of differing types of costs. Separate work packages should not be raised for different cost types. Within earned value management systems, specific terms are used to denote types of budgets, and each area of the budget has specific inclusions/exclusions. Budgets (in terms of pounds, hours or other measurable units) should be allocated to every work package within each control account.

Budgets should separately identify labour, material, sub-contract and any other direct costs. Please refer to sections 4.6 and 4.15.

It is the summation of all budgeted work that forms the performance measurement baseline.

4.9 What is the contract budget baseline?

The contract budget baseline (CBB) is the total contract value minus the margin. The CBB represents the total budget of all authorised work for the contract comprising the management reserve (MR) and PMB. This should equal the sum of the authorised budgets.

Generally, the CBB is fixed throughout the duration of the project, unless amended through contractual change.

4.10 What is management reserve?

MR is a portion of the CBB. It is held separately for future allocation to control accounts and will be used, if required, to cover increased work-scope requirements due to any unforeseen changes that fall within the overall scope of the contract.

Management reserve must never be used to eliminate past or current cost or schedule variances. This does not preclude allocation of reserve to future efforts in problem areas if the project manager agrees there is due cause.

Management reserve should not be used for changes in work scope originating from the customer. These are covered by contract amendments with agreed prices. The CBB is then increased to reflect the changes in work scope and budget.

4.11 What is performance measurement baseline?

The PMB is the time-phased budget plan, representing all budgets against which the contract performance (cost and schedule) is measured, spread across the planned duration of the project. It is equal to the total allocated budget less management reserve, and is represented as the BCWS.

The PMB consists of undistributed budget (UB) and distributed budget (DB):

$$PMB = UB + DB$$

4.12 What is undistributed budget?

UB is an amount within the PMB which is identified to a defined scope of work, but which has not yet been allocated to control accounts. As work is defined and assigned to control accounts, the UB should be reduced accordingly.

Undistributed budget is allocated primarily to accommodate temporary situations until control accounts can be agreed, or where contract requirements can be defined only in very general terms.

Procedures should be in place to ensure that UB set aside for specific but unallocated work is not distributed elsewhere.

4.13 What is distributed budget?

Distributed budget (DB) is allocated to control accounts and will form the majority of budgets within the PMB.

4.14 What is a performance measurement technique and earned value technique?

Performance measurement techniques are the methods used to estimate earned value. Different methods are appropriate to different work packages, either due to the nature of work or due to the planned duration of the work package.

Earned Value technique (EVT) is the technique to objectively assess progress. See Attribute 13, page 22.

4.15 The structure of budget elements on a project to calculate the cost of individual elements

Budgeting is the process of distributing or allocating cost targets to individual segments of work. Strict budget element relationships should exist at all times in order to ensure that the sum of the parts is equal to the whole. The hierarchy of budget elements is shown in Figure 12 below.

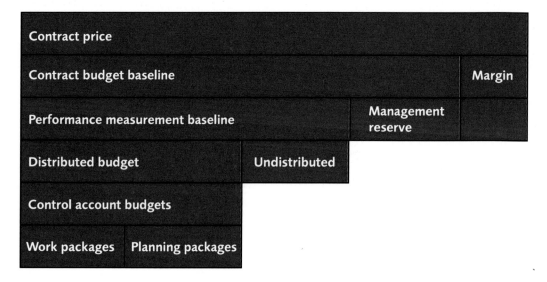

Figure 12: Budget element hierarchy
Taken from the *Earned Value Management: APM Guidelines* (2008)

This shows how the intermediate summations are defined leading to the contract budget base.

Within EVM systems, specific terms are used to denote types of budgets and each area of the budget has specific inclusions/exclusions. Specifically, the relationship between management reserve (MR) and the various contingencies should be auditable and controlled.

The project budget is maintained as a working management tool for the life of the project. The initial project budget is normally tied directly to the negotiated contract cost or internal management goals. The MR may be withheld before it is distributed to CAs. This should be done in one of two ways:

1. for MR that has already been allocated to a specific risk, this can be placed directly into the DB of the relevant CA.
2. Where non-specific risk provision is used, this should be moved from MR into UB and then into DB by using the appropriate change control process adopted by the project.

The budget will change as contract changes are authorised and incorporated or as internal re-planning actions are taken. Hourly charging rate changes and economic price adjustments may also be made as appropriate which will affect the budget elements. The project budget, at any level and for any organisation or task, will only contain budget for specific authorised work.

Projects usually involve many different types of costs that need to be summarised through various levels of detail. As WPs are sub-divisions of work, then each WP will comprise a number of different types of costs. Separate WPs should be raised for different cost types/elements in terms of money, hours or other measurable units within each CA. Budgets should independently identify labour, material, sub-contract, and any other direct costs. It is the summation of all budgeted work that forms the performance measurement baseline (PMB).

The project may include a number of options for the structure of the labour rates that will be applied to the budgets. The terms of the contract may dictate the rates to be used (for reporting), and any escalation assumptions. Within the project there should also be a defined process for the incorporation of labour rate changes, both on the actual costs and on the remaining budget. Irrespective of the method used, it is essential that both the budgeted cost of work performed (BCWP) and budgeted cost for work scheduled (BCWS) are based on the same budget rate for the PMB.

4.16 The possible impact of funding changes on the plan

Funding represents the money available from the company or the customer, and as such is subject to external commercial constraints.

Changes to projected funding may include:

- amount available;
- time-phasing of funding availability.

In these cases, the budget and associated work and schedule may be subject to change.

4.17 The importance of objective measures of performance

The key to performance measurement is the objective assessment of work in progress. All work is completed, in progress or not yet started.

Completed work presents no performance measurement problem, since these work packages have been closed. Future work will not be measured until the work gets under way. The only work packages to be concerned about are those that are planned to be or are actually in progress at the end of the reporting period. The difficulty of assessment of those packages will lie largely in the level of detail and the earnings method that has been selected.

If the earnings method is objective and is tied to schedule activities, then the job is straightforward and can be automated. If the earnings method is subjective or tied to events denoting a percentage completion, then a manual assessment will be necessary while a work package is in progress (also referred to as being 'open').

Judgements have to be made every reporting cycle from analysis by the project team on aspects of achievement, risk status and work to complete. Short work packages will make the assessment of achievement easier, but do not introduce arbitrary breaks in job planning and scheduling to shorten the work package duration as this goes against the objectiveness goal of EVM.

4.18 The standard methods of measuring earned value and their appropriate use

There are several approaches or methods of measuring earned value, known as earned value techniques (EVTs). The method used is dependent on the type of work being performed. Although a mixture of methods can be used on a single project, a work package or activity can be assigned only a single method. Once the work package has been opened, the method should not be changed.

Assignment of the EVT should be made at the work package level and consolidated through the WBS and OBS up to the total project level. Measurement of performance should be taken at the lowest practicable level to support the EVT. The following sections highlight some of the commonly used methods. It should be remembered that hybrid methods can be developed, as long as they are objective, and representative of the way that the work is planned to be undertaken.

4.18.1 Complete 0/100
The BCWP is earned only when the WP is complete; there is no partial earning for starting the WP.

4.18.2 Start/finish 50/50 and 20/80
If the activity has started and/or been completed, the percentage of the total budget/resources associated with the start/completion event is earned.

4.18.3 Percentage complete (Physical percent complete)
Percent complete is based on using various methods to discretely measure the progress for individual elements of work within the WP.

Earned value is determined by the CAM's assessment of work in progress. This technique may be applied to activities with duration spanning three or more reporting periods and **where an objective basis exists for determining percentage complete for the work package.**

4.18.4 Equivalent units
This method is based on measuring the number of units or items that have been completed and comparing the result with the total number of units or items that have to be completed.

This approach is normally used in manufacturing, where the BCWP is measured as the number of units produced – for example, if large quantities of a particular item are being produced. This method is not particularly suited to development activity unless it has a repetitive element.

4.18.5 Production (earned standards) technique
This technique is an objective variation of percent complete. It bases the EV claimed on a pre-determined value for a standard set of operations. As the operations are completed the associated BCWS is earned and reported (BCWP).

4.18.6 Milestones complete

Achievement of the work package is measured by the achievement of milestones.

Each milestone is assigned a proportion of the budget, and when the milestone is achieved, that proportion of the budget has been earned. This method of calculating earned value works best when there are a large number of frequent milestones. Earned value is only taken on milestone completion. If the number of milestones is low, then the measuring process becomes too coarse and is no longer useful to the project manager.

4.18.7 Formula method

The formula method is used where performance for low-value/non-critical material and other direct cost categories can be earned on the basis of actual cost, multiplied by the relationship of the budget at completion (BAC) to the EAC:

$$BCWP = ACWP \times BAC/EAC$$

This relies on a monthly update of the EAC to be accurate. It is useful in situations where progress can genuinely be directly related to spend – e.g. consumables, direct line feed. Table 9 provides examples of BCWP after applying the formula method based on a BAC value of 1,000 units.

Month	1	2	3	4	5
ACWP	200	400	700	1,000	1,400
EAC	1,000	1,000	1,200	1,300	1.400
BCWP	200	400	583	769	1,000

Table 9: Budgeted Cost for Work Performed calculations based on the formula method
Taken from the *Earned Value Management: APM Guidelines* (2008)

4.18.8 Management judgement (of percent complete)

In this case, BCWP is calculated based on the CAM's assessment of what percentage of the total work of the task has been completed. The CAM updates the estimate to reflect further progress in each period.

4.18.9 Level of effort

Level of effort (LoE) work packages are those within a project which are necessary for the project to be successful, but which do not have a specific end result or product and are not directly related to the generation of a specific result or product. Possible examples of such activities include some aspects of project management and contract administration. However, many of these activities, e.g. quality assurance and configuration management, should use the apportioned effort earned value technique (section 4.18.10).

Since LoE earned value is measured by the passage of time, it is important to ensure that the time-phased budget distribution is representative of the baseline schedule. Thus the achievement of the BCWP is always set equal to the BCWS, even if the work package has not started. This means schedule variances never occur, and hence LoE tasks do not allow meaningful earned value schedule analysis to be carried out.

However, LoE work packages can generate a cost variance (CV), and recorded ACWP can still be meaningfully compared with the BCWP.

LoE work packages should be separately defined from other work packages to avoid distorting any earned value analysis.

The LoE technique should be used only for those activities where no recovery action would be taken if the work were not undertaken.

4.18.10 Apportioned effort

Apportioned effort is effort that by itself is not readily divisible into short packages but is directly related to, and dependent upon, measurable progress within another work package.

Apportioned effort is normally used for tasks such as inspection (during manufacturing). The link between an apportioned account and a base account is a schedule link: this means that the schedule in the apportioned account is derived by analogy to the work schedule of the base account, and the earnings in the apportioned account are derived by analogy to the work accomplished in the base account.

Earned value is determined by an apportioned factor (AF) calculated from the BAC for the apportioned and reference work package. The apportioned BCWS and apportioned BCWP is calculated by applying the apportionment factor as follows:

apportioned BCWS = reference work package BCWS x AF

apportioned BCWP = reference work package BCWP x AF

There is no similar apportionment of ACWP values for apportioned effort type work packages. Actual costs are directly recorded and reported against the work package, resulting in the generation of cost variances where they exist. Hence:

ACWP = actual cost incurred from accounting system

The control account manager of the apportioned account still controls the assignment of budget to the account, but the time-phasing of that budget and the percentage of earnings are driven by the base account.

The use of apportioned effort is demonstrated in Table 10.

Reference work package	BCWS	0	60	120	210	
	BCWP	0	0	60	120	210
	ACWP	0	30	70	120	250
Apportioned work package AF = 0.33	BCWS	0	20	40	70	
	BCWP	0	0	20	40	70
	ACWP	0	10	40	50	65

Table 10: Apportioned work package calculations based on AF = 0.33
Taken from the *Earned Value Management: APM Guidelines* (2008)

4.19 The principles for progress measurement of materials

Earned value measurement for material is measured like any other element of cost. It is thus intended to permit assessment of events that reflect progress in project performance, not measurement of administrative or financial events (e.g. booking of actual costs or invoice payment). Therefore, BCWS should normally be scheduled in accordance with a project event and BCWP should be earned when the event occurs. Administrative or financial events may be used as indicators for contract events when such indicators occur in the same reporting period as the contract events.

4.20 The processes needed to establish an effective performance measurement baseline

The performance measurement baseline (PMB) forms the basis for measuring all future progress and performance, and consequently enables the project to be managed. The following steps will ensure that the PMB is aligned with the master schedule objectives and contract milestones:

* review the project requirements and establish key deliverables and risks;
* develop a WBS;
* develop an organisation breakdown structure (OBS);
* generate a responsibility assignment matrix (RAM), identifying CAs;
* produce WBS dictionary statements for each WBS element, to the lowest appropriate level (for example, WPs and PPs);
* determine and agree the EVM requirements for sub-contracts;
* identify master milestones and deliverables;
* develop the schedule for the duration of all activities and milestones. These should meet the customer/project requirement dates and be logically linked;
* group the activities to WPs and PPs;
* allocate resources (labour, material, sub-contracts and other direct costs) to activities;
* run a critical path to ensure the PMB runs continuously from the first activity to the last activity and check for other critical paths and the critical path drivers;
* when the dates are deemed satisfactory take a subset of the schedule, including the critical paths, and conduct a schedule risk analysis (SRA) incorporating uncertainty and appropriately identified risks;
* review the SRA outputs and determine if the customer/project requirement dates are still met; if not take appropriate action (mitigation activity, additional resources/sub-contract), and re-run the SRA to confirm schedule dates can be achieved;
* distribute the appropriate budgets across the WPs and PPs contained within the CAs;
* determine and assign the appropriate EVT for the WPs;
* establish the PMB under configuration control.

Initially the PMB value identified by the project manager may contain a significant amount of undistributed budget UB). This will be determined by the size, length and complexity of the project. As work-scope becomes more fully defined and CAs are approved, the DB increases by the value of the approved SoW and the UB is in turn reduced.

Periodic progress updates should be used to record progress, not to update and change the plan. All project team members should be actively using and reporting against a common plan. Any changes to the PMB should undergo a formal approval process before they form part of the baseline plan.

The key to having a proper management system is to ensure that the baseline plan represents the authorised execution for the Project. This may be achieved by conducting an Integrated Baseline Review (IBR).

4.21 The principles of risk planning

This section details a set of principles for planning and estimating the cost and time impacts for those risks that are deemed by analysis to be critical, significant or relevant to the project. The project manager will need to know that the initial risk impacts of, for example, six months and £1 million, are linked to a specific risk and have been generated accurately. In addition, the project manager needs to know the latest estimates and recovery plans should the risk(s) materialise.

This section demonstrates how these risk impacts should be reconciled with the management reserve (MR) once they have been agreed. It provides details on the processes by which these impacts can be derived for residual risk impacts and for planning risk mitigation actions. It also identifies how these should be reconciled with the residual risk impacts and the project's MR. In addition, it sets out the process for implementing fallback controls in the performance measurement baseline (PMB).

The risk planning section also describes how to ensure that planning principles are used to:

- generate estimates for time and cost impacts for specific project risks that are held in the project risk register;
- generate estimates for fallback control actions before adding these to the PMB;
- generate estimates for risk mitigation action(s) before adding these to the PMB;
- ensure that the correct EVTs have been applied to risk mitigation actions and fallback control actions within the PMB.

Why does risk planning need to be done?

- To enable a more robust generation of the cost and schedule reserve for technical and managerial risks for the whole project.
- To support the reconciliation of budgets and work between the PMB and MR.
- To avoid the double-counting of budget used for MR and mitigation action when creating the PMB and the risk appetite for the project.
- To enable a more robust defence of the level of MR required for specific technical and managerial risks.
- To help provide a more stringent estimate of residual risk impact for risks in the project risk register.
- To help provide benchmarks for future project risk planning.

4.21.1 Initiate risk planning

Inputs
The following is a list of project documentation that will be beneficial in risk planning:

- project risks with initial quantitative and qualitative estimates for risk impacts;
- initial plans for risk fallbacks and mitigation actions;
- estimating norms or benchmarks where these exist, from previous projects or project risk registers;
- a list of the project assumptions;
- the project schedule;
- planning and risk management software to conduct the cost risk analysis (CRA) and schedule risk analysis (SRA);
- the items of legislation and regulation(s) that must be complied with (statute law) and those that have been cited in the project contract, where applicable.

Methods
Estimating risk impacts for time and cost:

- capture the risk impact SoW. List the activities that need to be done to recover from the risk impact;
- include all compliance, assurance and quality control activities;
- start to identify owners for each activity;
- identify the final activity that will enable the entire recovery plan to be signed off and closed;
- identify the products or deliverables that must be included in the plan;
- ensure that controls are identified as well as recovery actions;
- identify the logical links between each activity;
- add resources to each activity, plus three point estimates;

- identify any secondary risks that may prevent the objectives in the recovery plan from being achieved. Update the risk breakdown structure (RBS) as appropriate;
- ensure that any reviews and post-recovery evaluations are included in the plan as required;
- run this schedule through the project's CRA/SRA application;
- capture the minimum, maximum and most likely time and cost impacts in the risk register – these are the new current risk impact values;
- re-run the project CRA/SRA with the new risk impacts;
- reconcile the new project cost and time reserves with the current MR – consider raising change control notes if required by the project's change control process (and the guidance in the Change management section 7.7 on page 118);
- reconcile the individual expected monetary value (EMV) for the individual risk with the MR, if the risk is still deemed to be critical, significant or relevant.

Outputs

At the end of the risk planning process the following should be updated/completed:

- a risk recovery schedule including costs and timescales.
- qualitative values in the risk register for individual risks.
- reconciled EMV for individual risks.
- cost and schedule reserve values.
- the RBS.

4.21.2 Planning the risk mitigation activities for specific risks

Inputs

The following is a list of project documentation that will be beneficial in planning risk mitigation activities:

- mitigation actions from specific risks in the risk register.
- the current schedule.

Methods

- Identify the end activity or milestone that will ensure completion of the mitigation activity.
- From the risk mitigation action, identify the key activities that are required.
- If the mitigation action has more than one activity, capture the logical links between each one.
- Allocate resources to each task/activity and select an EVT for each one, depending on the criteria set out in section 4.22 on page 71.
- Identify the best place in the schedule for the mitigation activity/task.
- Follow the change control process to introduce the tasks/activities.
- Incorporate activities into the schedule and WP dictionary once they are approved.
- Update the RAM as necessary.
- Capture dates for mitigation completion and transfer to the risk register.
- Update the risk waterfall chart with relevant dates that align with the reduction in cost and/or time impacts.
- Update the time/cost impact plan mentioned above.

Outputs

At the end of the risk mitigation process the following should be updated/completed:

- schedule;
- WP dictionary;
- time/cost impact plan;
- waterfall chart;
- lessons learnt log;
- the PBS, WBS and RAM.

4.21.3 Fallback controls if specific risks happen

Fallback controls are a specific type of mitigation action that needs to be put in place during this stage. The output of this action is then used to start the fallback action should the risk impact.

For example, the risk of disruption to business due to flooding at an electricity generating station has been identified. Mitigation actions are implemented following a cost/benefit analysis of these actions in order to minimise the probability and/or impact of flooding at the station. In the event that the station is flooded, the risk manager has identified the need for a fallback plan. This includes a process for shutting down and evacuating the station in a controlled manner. It also needs to include a business continuity plan to ensure that other generating stations nearby can supply electricity while this station is offline.

The fallback control action in this instance may be a document and it would include:

- what needs to be done by whom;
- when and in what order;
- how to evacuate the site;

- how to shut it down;
- who needs to communicate what to which stakeholder.

Methods

The method shown for generating risk mitigation actions should be used.

Outputs

At the end of this process, the following should be updated/completed:

- risk fallback control activities;
- schedule;
- risk register;
- change control log;
- lessons learned log;
- work package dictionary;
- PBS, WBS and RAM.

4.22 Appropriate earned value techniques for different types of work package

EV is the technique used to measure achievement; also known as the budgeted cost of work performed (BCWP). The EVT chosen must best represent the effort required and provide the most appropriate method for planning and scheduling as well as evaluating performance.

There should be only one EVT per work package. Responsibility for the selection of the EVT lies with the control account manager (CAM), who may obtain assistance from the WP manager or the project co-ordinator. Ultimate approval of all EVTs used on a project lies with the project manager. The EVTs available can be constrained by the scheduling tool being used.

There are three types of work package:

1. **discrete** – tasks where there is a tangible product or a verifiable outcome that can be directly planned and measured.

2. **level of effort** – unmeasured effort, usually of a supportive nature and possibly without a deliverable end product. Examples are supervision, programme and contract administration.

3. **apportioned** – effort that is not readily measured or divisible into discrete WPs but which is directly related to the planning and performance on other measured (i.e. discrete) effort.

The vast majority of WPs on a project should be the discrete type. The 0/100, milestones or quantifiable percentage complete EVTs are objective measures of the value in progress work and are likely to provide the best match to the estimated resource profile.

4.22.1 Discrete effort

The following methods are ordered according to the degree of objectivity they provide from the most objective (first) to the least objective (last).

Method	Application guide
0/100	Work packages that are planned to be one reporting period or less in duration.
Start/finish 50/50 and 20/80	Work packages that span two reporting periods or more in duration. For those work packages that are more than one (or span more than one) reporting period in duration, the weighting of the start and completion milestones should be a reflection of the resources that are scheduled in the month.
Percentage complete (Physical percent complete)	Whilst typically used on work packages lasting longer than one reporting period, it is important that the activities within the work package are of short duration (i.e. a reporting period or less). The elements of work must be measurable and quantifiable (e.g. metres cubed of concrete poured, or number of tests completed); it must be possible to produce evidence to justify the percent complete. For example, in the production of a document, 70% for document written, 80% when reviewed, 90% when approved, 100% when stored in the document repository.
Equivalent units complete	This technique is available to any work package where the output is comprised of similar units. It is an objective variation of percent complete that bases the earned value claimed on a pre-determined value for a number of completed production units. For example, for a work package that produces 40 drawings that are of similar effort, the completion of 30 drawings translates to 75% complete, just as having produced 30 like assemblies out of a total of 40 that are planned).
Production (earned standards) technique	This is applicable only to the manufacture of a product or assembly. These manufacturing activities while not projects in their own right can form part of an overall project.
Milestone	For efforts of two or more reporting periods in duration, interim milestones with their own achievement criteria representing work accomplishment are required — two per month is ideal. However the minimum target is that there is at least one milestone per reporting period, unless there is nothing tangible to measure.
Quantifiable	This technique can be applied to a WP of any duration, but it is generally used for work packages more than two reporting periods in duration. Normally there would be associated rules of credit.
Management judgement (of percent complete)	This technique may be used for work packages more than two periods in duration where the milestone technique isn't applicable.

4.22.2 Level of effort

Level of effort	Level of effort tasks have no product or accomplishment criteria associated with them and therefore they either cannot be measured or it is impracticable to measure them on any basis other than the passage of time.

4.22.3 Apportioned

Apportioned effort	Used where there is no measurable output but there is a direct performance relationship to another discrete activity. Preferred to level of effort, if the declared proportionality can be substantiated.

Table 11: Table of methods/effort
Reproduced with kind permission from General Dynamics UK.

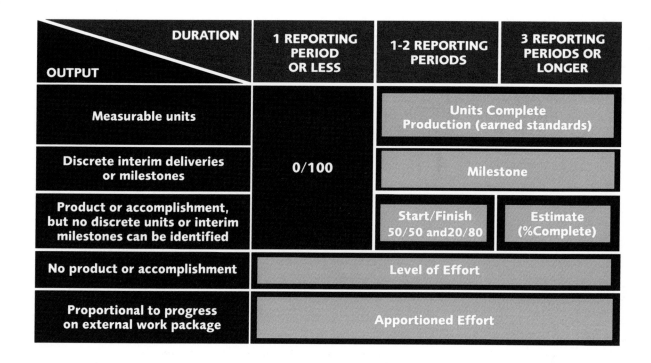

OUTPUT \ DURATION	1 REPORTING PERIOD OR LESS	1-2 REPORTING PERIODS	3 REPORTING PERIODS OR LONGER
Measurable units		Units Complete Production (earned standards)	
Discrete interim deliveries or milestones	0/100	Milestone	
Product or accomplishment, but no discrete units or interim milestones can be identified		Start/Finish 50/50 and 20/80	Estimate (%Complete)
No product or accomplishment	Level of Effort		
Proportional to progress on external work package	Apportioned Effort		

Figure 13: Summary of EVT applicability
Reproduced with kind permission from General Dynamics UK Ltd

4.23 The validity and likely effectiveness of a plan

To test if a plan is valid and effective there are a number of approaches that can be taken:

* an assessment using the *Earned Value Management Compass* model (APM, 2010);
* an integrated baseline review;
* data trace assessment.

4.23.1 Earned Value Management Compass model
The *Earned Value Management (EVM) Compass* maturity model (APM, 2010) provides a defined means of establishing and improving project control capability. The review is conducted using a maturity grid that outlines performance levels rated on a scale of 1–5, with five being the highest, against 25 attributes of an EVM system. A realistic and evidenced-based approach needs to be taken to make the review beneficial. To satisfy a requirement for ANSI 748 compliance maturity level scores will need to be above three in all categories.

4.23.2 Integrated baseline review
An integrated baseline review (IBR) is a formal review conducted by an independent team or customer and tests the establishment of the technical, cost and schedule baselines. Correctly executed, it is the most comprehensive of all the reviews and should:

* cover CAMs;
* determine the credibility, sufficiency and adequacy of the planning;
* ensure that activities are integrated with each other;
* focus on the risks.

This method of review includes interviews with the managers (primarily CAMs) led by subject specialists and supported by EV experts. The IBR should include participation by technical specialists who are capable of ascertaining and evaluating the technical aspects, schedule and cost risks, as well as whether the baseline properly reflects those risks.

The IBR should be held as soon as possible after the project has completed a minimum of one reporting cycle, but ideally three reporting cycles, following the establishment of the initial baseline. This ensures that performance data is available during the review.

4.23.3 Data trace assessment
Data traces form part of the IBR but can also be used for an independent assessment. The traces will sample some of the CAM's data and will give a good indication of the validity and effectiveness of a plan. Areas to review include:

4.23.3.1 Organisation/authorisation
The organisation/authorisation trace shows the progressive breakdown of a discrete piece of work from the contract to, at least the CA, and usually to a lower level.

It is suggested that the following documentation, appropriately authorised and signed, should be reviewed:

* a page of the contract;
* programme authorisation, if appropriate;
* functional authorisations, if appropriate;
* RAM;
* CA/SoW;
* CAP. If appropriate there may be lower levels of authorisation, such as WP authorisation. If they exist they should be included as part of the trace.

For the selected WPs or activities associated with work scope, authorisation and responsibilities, the following actions need to be taken:

* select a CA and data trace item by reviewing the WBS and WBS dictionary and ensure they adequately define the contractual effort to be achieved within the CA. Check this against the SoW and ensure all references match. Add comments to the WBS and WBS dictionary pages to indicate the contract line item and end item elements relating to the CA that you are tracing;
* review the RAM to locate the CA which contains the trace item. Ensure that this CA is assigned to the correct OBS element that is consistent with the effort to be accomplished. Annotate the RAM to indicate that the CA was developed at the intersection of the WBS to the organisational structure and that the WBS was extended down to CA level;
* review the work authorisation documents for the CA which contains the trace item. Verify that the OBS assigned in the RAM matches the OBS in the work authorisation documents. Ensure that the work authorisation documents are approved and signed by the relevant managers designated in the RAM. Ensure that the work authorisation and WBS definitions of the effort to be achieved within the CA are consistent. Provide the CA work authorisation documents as exhibits;
* review CA/WP schedules which contain the trace item. Ensure that they are compatible with the effective dates on the work authorisation documents for that CA.

4.23.3.2 Budgeting
The budget trace confirms the integrity of the budget baseline, starting with the contract price and finishing with detailed time-phased baseline budgets for each WP. The budget trace should identify both static and dynamic integrity. For example, it should show the current month's status plus any documented changes to the baseline.

For the selected WPs or activities associated with budgeting, the following should be done:

- review the WP planning sheets for the control account (CA) which contains the items. Confirm that these plans reflect the way in which work is to be done, that there are an appropriate number of WPs versus PPs, and that the PPs are neither too general nor too large in scope, value and duration;
- review the CA documentation and internal reports as they relate to the trace items. Ensure that the sum of the PP budgets plus the WP budgets equals the cost-account budget on the responsibility assignment matrix (RAM). Ensure that the PPs have their own budget values and that there are adequate procedures for converting a PP into a WP. Check this against the basis of estimate (BoE) for the work and note any inconsistencies;
- locate the trace item in the bill of materials (BoM) and/or purchase order, if applicable. Check for consistency and highlight any inconsistencies;
- review WP planning sheets and other performance measurement reports for the CA which contain the trace item. Determine how the budgeted cost of work scheduled (BCWS) was time phased and established;
- review the budget information in the work authorisation documents, the RAM, and the internal performance measurement reports to ensure that they are reconcilable. Then check that the amounts in the internal cost performance report are consistent with any external reports.

4.23.3.3 Schedule

The schedule trace should establish the total schedule process from planning, establishing the baseline, the schedule update process, to the baseline change process.

The actual schedule trace should begin with the deliverables including dates, which form part of the contract. All contractual and payment milestones, design reviews and sub-contractor deliverables should form part of the master programme schedule.

For the selected WPs or activities associated with scheduling:

- review the CA/WP schedules;
- confirm that the schedule contains all contractual activities. Compare this against the price and delivery schedule for consistency;
- complete a vertical schedule trace which shows the flow from these schedules, through the intermediate schedules, to the master schedules;
- complete a horizontal trace which shows that the appropriate CAs and WPs are linked in a logical way;
- check that the time-phased budget (BCWS) for the same WPs are consistent with the start and finish dates on the baseline schedule;
- check that the CA or the WBS element start and finish dates on the CA plans are consistent with both the BCWS baseline spread and the baseline schedule;
- confirm the identification of work progress and forecast of completion dates, if appropriate. Check that the latest schedule status has been reflected in the revised schedule.

4.23.3.4 Resources

The resource trace should confirm that the required resources, including budgets, facilities, personnel, skills, etc. one match the required availability. It should also be sufficient to achieve the technical SoW within the schedule constraints over the entire performance period. It is important to:

- check that all activities are resourced;
- determine if there is any evidence that smoothing of a resource has taken place;
- assess if the resource demand profiles are peaked/spiked;
- assess if the planned use of resources matches availability.

4.23.3.5 Sub-contract management
The sub-contract management trace should consider the following:

- is the responsibility for sub-contract management identified?
- how will the CAM verify sub-contractor progress and manage their performance?
- is the sub-contracted effort integrated into the CAM's schedules?
- is the earned value system enabling meaningful progress data to be reported?
- check to see how the sub-contracted effort is planned and that the EVT to be used to measure performance is appropriate. The BCWS should be based upon identifiable milestones where possible and the use of LoE should be minimised.
- ensure sub-contractor schedules are vertically and horizontally integrated with the CAM's schedules.
- check the process for tracking the material issued from the CAM to the sub-contractor and vice versa.
- check for proper incorporation of the sub-contractor's data into the CAM's system.
- ensure that the CAM's EAC includes sub-contractor updates for actual costs, material values, etc.

4.23.3.6 Earned value
The EV trace demonstrates the process for the collection of EV status and will normally consist of the following:

- do the CAs identify EVTs at work package level (or lower) to enable effective measurement of progress?
- review the LoE content of CA budgets to ensure it is only applied where appropriate. If possible obtain a summary of LoE accounts for the project;
- identify the percent complete figure and ensure that the CAM has objective measures to identify the progress at a lower level to prevent subjective progress measurement. There should be detailed tasks or WPs with identified discrete milestones;
- where progress has been claimed does it match the EVT identified?
- Check the CA status sheets to ensure that progress is being claimed appropriately. For example, a 0-100% EVT package should have zero progress until it is complete.

4.23.3.7 Managerial analysis
The managerial analysis trace will determine if the data is reliable and subsequent information useful for management decisions. It will normally check that:

- EV is being claimed in the same manner in which it was planned, for example, if an EVT of 0-100% is used, there should be no interim BCWP claimed.
- the estimate at completion (EAC) is being updated and providing meaningful indications of the likely outcomes.
- that any EAC reported reflects information to date. Check that cumulative variances are either explained and a corrective action plan is in place or the variance is reflected in the EAC.
- EAC includes amounts for completed CAs or WPs and ensure that the ACWP does not exceed the EAC. It should be equal as the work is complete and the EAC reflects the revised amount.
- are variance reports are being generated to enable effective management.
- variance analysis reports are reviewed to ensure the following:
  - the reasons for the variance are adequately explained, e.g. it should not simply say that there was a variance;
  - the impact is identified, e.g. how it affects other control accounts and whether it affects the programme overall;
  - corrective action or recovery plan is identified;
  - analysis is approved at a higher level than it is prepared.

4.23.3.8 Risk
The risk trace confirms that any risks are identified in the risk register and that the approval process is correctly authorised and monitored. The following should be reviewed:

- confirm what, if any, risks are identified within the risk register;
- schedule risk – review the SRA outputs and check how these align to the overall schedule dates. If there is a mismatch what mitigation activity is being planned?
- cost risk – the assessment should determine whether there is sufficient management reserve to address the risk items and assumptions identified.

5 Data collection

5.1 The types of data that should be collected

The *data collection* processes are concerned with ensuring that complete and accurate information is collected in a timely manner to enable the transfer of actual cost and progress information into the earned value management system. The actual cost of work performed (ACWP) used in the earned value calculations includes:

- labour costs (direct costs and indirect costs);
- direct expenses;
- material costs;
- subcontractor costs of work done;
- the budgeted cost of work performed (BCWP) information will be derived from the application of the agreed EVTs.

5.2 The appropriate frequency and level of detail for data collection

Performance data should be collected on a regular and scheduled basis, for example, daily, weekly or monthly, as appropriate for the project scale, its duration, risk, lifecycle stage and complexity.

Actual costs should be collected at a level that will identify the cost elements and factors contributing to cost variance. ACWP should be recorded in a manner consistent with the budget and should include all expenditure.

The level of collection should enable the appropriate visibility to management of cost performance without imposing an unnecessary administrative burden in terms of data collection.

As costs can be transferred or mis-booked during a period, it is recommended that cumulative costs be used in any calculations. Costs for the period should therefore be calculated as the difference between the cumulative costs last period and the current cumulative costs.

5.3 The importance of data integrity

Ensure that there are procedures in place to protect the integrity of bookings to WPs/CAs. For example the correct numbering system should be set up, based on the WBS, and correct booking/charge numbers should be available as required.

The estimated actuals process should be used when necessary to ensure there are no variances due to any payment delays.

The actual costs are verified to ensure only valid costs are booked to valid booking and charge numbers.

5.4 The need for BCWS, BCWP and ACWP to relate to the same timeframe

Ensure that the BCWS, the BCWP and the ACWP are created in the same timeframe. It may not be possible to ensure that EV is claimed in the same period that actual costs are applied but in these cases, the company may choose to use estimated actual costs (or accruals) in the EVMS, and the associated reports. A procedure should be in place to cover the process, and the subsequent replacement with the real costs.

5.5 When is it appropriate to use estimated actuals and/or accruals?

Estimated actuals (adjustments to actual costs)

During the execution of a project, work will be completed or goods delivered for which BCWP has been claimed, but the associated actual cost has not been recognised in the accounting system. This creates a payment lag.

Doing nothing would mask the true cost performance and cause favourable variances to be reported where the ACWP is used in the calculation, for example, cost variance (CV), cost performance index (CPI) and independent estimate at completion (IEAC) calculations. This may lead to ill-informed decision making. However, the use of estimated actuals will mitigate these false variances by reflecting a more accurate and meaningful ACWP.

When a change is made to ACWP, the following should be noted:

* the basis of the estimate should be objective, such as the price from an invoice, purchase order, vendor quote or estimated hours and rates;
* document the change to explain why the ACWP is at a variance to the accounting system;
* ensure that when the real cost is recorded in a later reporting period within the accounting system, the estimated actual is reversed out of the ACWP in that same reporting period. In accounting terms an estimated actual is similar to an accrual.
* Invoicing a customer inclusive of estimated actuals is not allowed.

Estimated actuals need not always be positive. There will be situations where they can be legitimately used negatively, for example, incorrect cost assignment where costs have been mistakenly posted to the project which will be reporting too high an ACWP. There will now be an adverse cost variance causing needless Variance Analysis Report (VAR) explanations, so estimated actuals can also be applied. Estimated actuals should be documented and action taken to reverse the incorrect costs in the company's accounting system as soon as possible.

Estimated actuals should not be used for every small discrepancy found in the ACWP, but when used appropriately, they will increase the integrity of a project's reported performance. Examples of common usage are when dealing with high value material, hardware and finished goods and services.

5.6 Defining effective data collection requirements for a specific project and organisation

Whether data collection is completed manually or automatically, there will always be errors in any data collection system. The errors rise with the number of people and transactions involved. Particular attention should be given to:

* how easy is it to enter data accurately?
* how are data errors dealt with?
* how are non-bookings dealt with?
* is there enough capacity to process all the data in a timely fashion?

5.6.1 Considerations for data collection

- What data is required?
- How much data is required?
- Is the data available in the required format?
- How is the data gathered at the collection point?
- Where is the data collected?
- How is the data recorded?
- How is the data checked, corrected and authorised?
- How often is the data collected?
- Are there enough collection points to gather the data in a timely fashion?
- Is the data being used appropriately?

5.7 Verifying, validating and reconciling data integrity

Once data has been collected, the verification and validation activities need to be undertaken to ensure that the data is accurate and error-free, and that the measures of performance are still valid from when it was established. Where errors are identified it is important that they be corrected to ensure that data presented through management reports presents a true reflection of performance and does not lead to unnecessary variance analysis, where the variance is in fact an issue with the data.

CAMs will perform data verification checks to ensure that the data collected is an accurate reflection of the work performed in the period and that it is recorded against the appropriate work. Typical verification checks will include:

- BCWP – checking that performance claimed is in line with expectations and the EVT that was selected to reflect performance;
- ACWP – ensuring that the booking made against the project's WPs are in line with what was expected (both in terms of what has been booked and where it has been booked);
- EAC – checking that the EAC is realistic based upon the performance achieved to date. This should be supported by measures such as TCPI and independent EAC calculations.

Validation checks will also be completed to ensure that the data is appropriate and that it meets the original data requirements. A typical example would be to review the EVT used for an element of work and ensure that it was appropriate to the type of work completed and how it was delivered.

Where errors are identified it is important that they are corrected as soon as possible, ideally within the same reporting period. Where BCWP has been incorrectly claimed this will usually be resolved in discussions with the party that recorded the data.

With ACWP, errors will usually be corrected in agreement with both the party that posted the cost and the party that will receive the cost when the correction is made. This may result in either inter-project or intra-project cost transfers and should involve the appropriate staff from within an organisation to effect the change.

Where data is not corrected within a certain period, it should be corrected as soon as possible. At no point should the error be corrected in the historical EV dataset as this will distort EVM performance data and conceal the cause of the variance within the current period data.

6 Analysis, review and action

6.1 The formulae for earned value variance and indices

All variances are measured in terms of cost and apply equally to all methods of measurement. There are five types of variances/ indices commonly used.

SV   **Schedule variance** – the cost comparison of what has been earned with what was budgeted. It measures the difference in value between the work planned and the work actually accomplished:

$$SV = BCWP - BCWS$$
$$SV\% = (SV/BCWS) \times 100$$

CV   **Cost variance** – the cost comparison of what has been earned with what has been spent:

$$CV = BCWP - ACWP$$
$$CV\% = (CV/BCWP) \times 100$$

VAC   **Variance at completion** – the cost comparison of the budget at completion with the current estimate at completion:

$$VAC = BAC - EAC$$
$$VAC\% = (VAC/BAC) \times 100$$

SPI   **Schedule performance index** – an indication of how far behind or ahead of the planned work the project is (in terms of the value of the work accomplished); it tends towards 1.0 as the project progresses. It is of less value as the project nears completion:

$$SPI = BCWP/BCWS$$

CPI   **Cost performance index** – the index of earned value to actual costs. Below 1.0 is unfavourable; above 1.0 is favourable:

$$CPI = BCWP/ACWP$$

In addition to these variances being shown on a cumulative spend graph, the indices can also be plotted cumulatively through the life of a project to show improving (or worsening) performance.

6.2 The difference between schedule status and earned value progress

It is essential to update the status of schedules in a timely manner to gain an objective understanding of the achievement of milestones and deliverables, and to monitor how task dependencies are affected by any task movement.

When updating the schedule status, the following should be considered:

- activity actual start/finish dates;
- estimate of time remaining to complete the task;
- estimated start and finish dates for future activities.

Schedule status may then be determined by comparing how much time the activity is ahead of or behind the baseline schedule.

The following aspects of schedule assessment may be performed at both detail and project level:

- review of the critical path activities;
- review of schedule against key milestone forecasts;
- review of future resource requirements.

6.3 Typical earned value reports, graphs and progress charts

6.3.1 Reporting graphs

Figure 14 demonstrates the performance of a project using the earned value data elements. It provides a quick view of project status and prevailing trends. It may be used as a basis for forecasting the project end conditions. It can also include, if required, the EAC and the forecast completion date for the previous reporting periods.

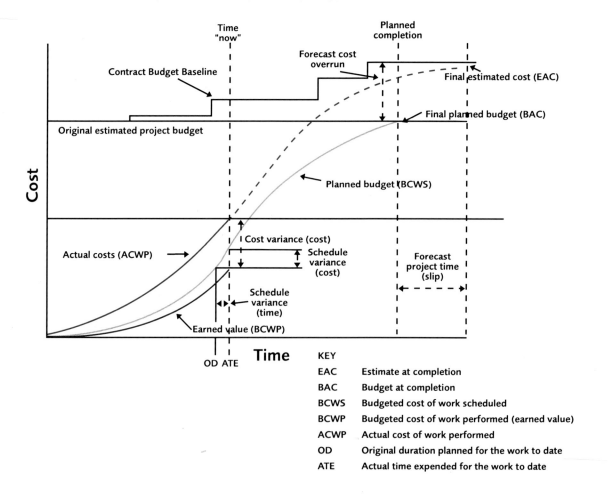

Figure 14: EV graph including trend analysis
Taken from the *Earned Value Management: APM Guidelines* (2008)

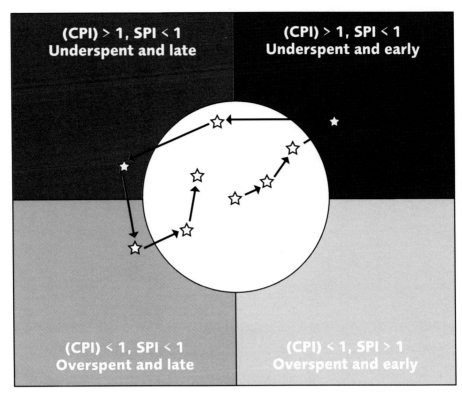

Figure 15: Bulls-eye chart
Taken from the *Earned Value Management: APM Guidelines* (2008)

6.3.2 Performance trend charts

The bulls-eye chart (Figure 15) shows the change in schedule performance index and cost performance index at each reporting period. The graph gives a summary view as to whether performance is improving or deteriorating and whether the variances are outside the agreed thresholds. The central circle shows the maximum variance thresholds. The CPI and SPI are plotted on the graph at each reporting cycle in the project.

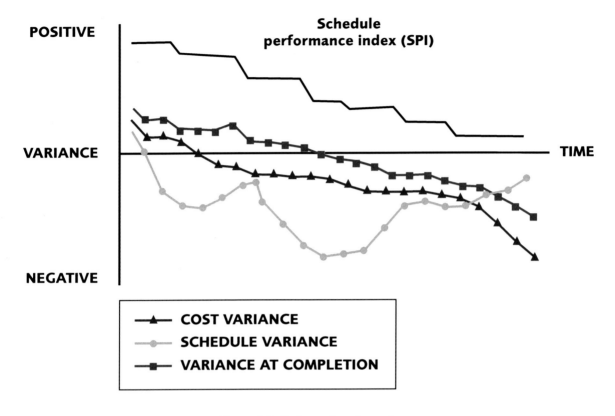

Figure 16: Variance trend graphs
Taken from the *Earned Value Management: APM Guidelines* (2008)

An alternative approach to the bulls-eye chart is to show the change in schedule variance and cost variance on a time phase. Such a graph (Figure 16) indicates whether performance is improving.

Another graph that can be used is the CPI/SPI curve that shows CPI and SPI on a time phase.

The assessment of performance through cost and schedule variance should take into account any potential 'washout' of any one budget type over another – e.g. where material cost is significantly higher than the cost of the labour required to process/ use the material. In these instances, separate work packages should be created for material and labour. Similarly, consideration should be given to the separation of level of effort and indirect cost elements from measured elements.

6.4 The principle of variance thresholds

It is strongly recommended that variance thresholds be established. This will ensure that not all variances need be printed or explained in detail at each reporting cycle. These thresholds are set to minimise the detail included in reports when there are only minor variances.

If any of the values being monitored fall within predefined limits then full details are not required on the variances. However, when any of the variances fall outside the thresholds then a full variance analysis, together with methods of recovery, should be reported.

Thresholds can be set as a value, as a percentage, or both. The values set for each project will be decided by the size, complexity, risk and so on of each project. It is normal for separate thresholds to be set for last reporting period and cumulative performance. Consideration should also be given to the convergence of thresholds over the life of the project.

6.5 The formulae for estimate at completion (EAC)

An estimate at completion (EAC) is the estimate of final cost based on realistic plans and assumptions by management and using the most current and accurate information available.

The EAC is the sum of the actual costs (ACWP) up to the present, plus the best estimates of the costs still to be incurred, (estimate to completion, ETC).

EACs are calculated and analysed at any level of the WBS or OBS. Thus:

EAC = actual costs incurred + remaining work
The basic formula is:
$EAC = ACWP_{cumulative} + ETC$

Where ETC is the estimate to completion
Or ETC = (BAC-BCWP)/PI
Where PI is a performance indicator, for example SPI, CPI or a combination of indices.

So $EAC = ACWP_{CUM} + (BAC-BCWP)/PI$
BAC = Budget at completion and BCWP is the budgeted cost of work performed – the earned value.

The EAC can also be calculated by using a simpler version of the above formula:

EAC = BAC/CPI

This does not take remaining work into account, it only uses the current BAC and the cumulative CPI, so may be seen as an extreme EAC calculation. It should therefore be used in conjunction with other EAC formulae to give an overall EAC range and trend.

The EAC calculation should be generated for each CA and for the entire project.

The following should be considered when defining a detailed EAC:

- past performance;
- required efficiency to recover;
- costs (incurred and committed) to date;
- the use of contract charging rates (incorporating overhead cost pools) to obtain the cost of labour based estimates;
- technical assessment of tasks remaining;
- cost and schedule variances incurred to date;
- expected future efficiency;
- percentage of task already completed and remaining risks (risk review and probability of cost impact);
- ongoing or outstanding management actions;
- forecast schedule completion of the task;
- anticipated changes to the scope of work;
- future economic conditions, forecast rate changes and escalation indices;
- Previous EAC trend.

6.6 The formulae for tests of reasonableness

Current performance indicators (SPI, CPI) will provide a 'performance to date' view of the project.

To complete performance index (TCPI) allows a projection of the anticipated performance to achieve either the BAC or the EAC (dependent on which formula is employed) – i.e., what level of performance needs to be achieved to meet the BAC or EAC.

TCPI(BAC) = (BAC-BCWP)/(BAC-ACWP) = work remaining/cost remaining

TCPI(EAC) = (BAC-BCWP)/(EAC-ACWP) = work remaining/estimated cost remaining
A figure greater than 1.0 indicates that future efficiency will need to be greater than planned, conversely less than 1.0 indicates future efficiency may be less than planned to achieve BAC or EAC (dependent on which formula is employed).

TCPI(BAC) should be compared with the CPI. This can provide additional performance information. If the TCPI(BAC) is greater than the current CPI, future efficiency must improve if the project is to achieve the BAC/EAC.

Period					
BCWS (PV)	1	2	3	4	5
BCWP (EV)	10	20	50	80	120
ACWP (AC)	10	115	20	60	100
BAC	11	20	30	80	110
EAC	120	120	120	120	120
CPI	0.91	0.75	0.67	0.75	0.91
TCPI (BAC)	1.01	1.05	1.11	1.50	2.00
TCPI (BAC)	0.91	0.75	0.67	0.75	0.91

Demonstrates the use of TCPI.

	Period				
	1	2	3	4	
BCWS (PV)	10	20	50	80	12
BCWP (EV)	10	15	20	60	10
ACWP (AC)	11	20	30	80	11
BAC	120	120	120	120	12
EAC	132	160	180	160	13
CPI	0.91	0.75	0.67	0.75	0.9
TCPI (BAC)	1.01	1.05	1.11	1.50	2.0
TCPI (EAC)	0.91	0.75	0.67	0.75	0.9

Table 12: Example of projecting anticipated performance using TCPI (BAC) and TCPI (EAC)
Modified from the *Earned Value Management: APM Guidelines* (2008)

In this example, for period 1 a TCPI (BAC) of 1.01 is required to complete the remainder of the work within the budget at completion. When this is compared with the current CPI of 0.91, it is clear that significant performance improvements are required if this is to be achieved. It may be seen by looking at period 3 data that the required performance improvement – current CPI of 0.67 to TCPI (BAC) 1.11 – is unachievable; this should prompt a re-evaluation of the viability of the EAC.

To corroborate the accuracy of forecasted costs there are two approaches:

EAC = BAC/CPI
ETC = (BAC – BCWP)/CPI
To check forecast completion dates (in weeks from project start):

forecast completion = original completion/SPI

6.7 Calculating and interpreting earned value variances and indices

EV variances and indices are used to inform the project manager, customer and client on the health of a project. These variances and indices can be based on historical data and forecasts, and can be either for a specific period or look cumulatively over the entire project. In addition, variances and indices can be calculated for both time and cost and there are variances and indices that use the project manager's estimates instead of those calculated automatically. The use of such estimates is encouraged, along with the need for the project team to understand where the project manager's estimate is in relation to the automatically generated indices. The important point to note is the ability to forecast completion dates and times; it is also important to look at the trends in variances and indices. This is the most likely time and cost of completion, if current performance does not change. The most used variances are included in the *Earned Value Management: APM Guidelines (APM, 2008)*.

Figure 17 shows some of the most popular variances used. It also highlights how thresholds have been applied. The thresholds are set either by the project steering board or the project manager. In addition, the threshold values may change throughout the project lifecycle, especially at the end of a stage or phase and when the project has been subject to a re-baselining activity.

The threshold should be set so that it is neither too sensitive nor too insensitive. If the IEAC is continually breached in every reporting period, then it is likely that it has been set too close to an ideal performance target, for example a CPI or SPI of 1.0.

Similarly, if it is clear that the threshold is never breached, and this situation continues for seven reporting periods, then the threshold value should be reset.

The threshold enables the project manager to report by exception and to use the EV data to drill-down into the project WBS. Once the cause has been identified, the project manager has a number of options available to try and improve performance:

- accelerate a task/activity;
- delay a task/activity;
- start a task/activity;
- stop a task/activity.

Figure 17: A graph showing six different independent estimates at completion

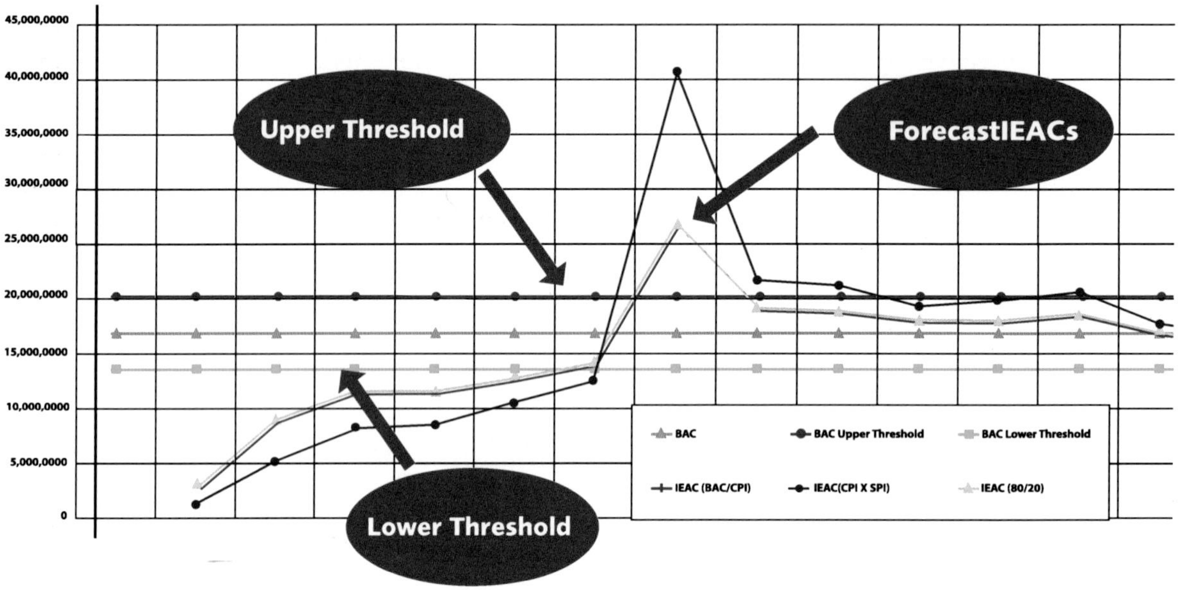

Reproduced with kind permission from the APM Planning, Monitoring and Control Specific Interest Group working group

EVM can be used as a predictor of project outcomes in terms of the final cost of the project. This is called the estimate at completion (EAC). There are many formulae that use past performance, (cost performance index (CPI), schedule performance index (SPI) or both), as indicators of future performance. Due to the use of formulae, the EAC is called an independent EAC (IEAC), i.e. there is no subjective judgement on the part of CAMs or project manager.

Examples of these IEACs are as follows:

$$IEAC = ACWP + ((BAC - BCWP) / (CPI \times SPI))$$
$$IEAC = BAC / CPI$$
$$IEAC = ACWP + ((BAC - BCWP) / ((CPI \times 0.8) + (SPI \times 0.2)))$$

However, using past performance to predict future outcomes may not be the best way of determining a project's EAC. The CAMs and project managers may have more information on the project's EAC based on influencing factors on the remaining work. This would be a more subjective view of the EAC.

When declaring a project's EAC, the project manager will have to take a balanced view by comparing the IEAC and the subjective EAC. If the EAC lies between the resultant IEAC calculations, then the project manager can gain confidence that it may be a reasonable estimate. To test whether a subjective EAC is reasonable, the project manager can apply a test by using the to complete performance indicator (TCPI) formula:

$$TCPI_{EAC} = (BAC - BCWP) / (EAC - ACWP)$$

This divides the remaining work, (numerator), by the amount of resources that are needed to meet the subjective EAC (denominator).

A value greater than 1.0 will indicate to the project manager that the project will have to perform more cost efficiently than it has in the past if the subjective EAC is to be reached. A $TCPI_{EAC}$ of 1.1 informs the project manager that the project will have to perform 10% more efficiently on the remaining work if it is going to reach the subjective EAC, therefore the EAC is likely to be understated and needs revising upwards.

The project manager can also use the CPI to help in their decision making process. As a rule of thumb, a project that has consistently been overspent, indicated by a CPI of less than 1.0, and a $TCPI_{EAC}$ of greater than 1.1, is unlikely to suddenly improve its cost efficiency in the future. It suggests the EAC is not sufficient, although every case will have to be examined on its own merits.

There is another TCPI formula, which is:

$$TCPI_{BAC} = (BAC - BCWP) / (BAC - ACWP)$$

This divides the remaining work, (numerator), by the amount of resources that are needed to meet the BAC (denominator).

This formula relates to how realistic the budget is. Again, if the $TCPI_{BAC}$ is 1.1, this informs the project manager that the project will have to perform 10% more efficiently on the remaining work if it is going to meet the BAC.

No one indicator will provide enough information for the project manager to make informed decisions. It is important for the project manager to observe trends, manage by exception using thresholds, and use all the information that an EVMS can generate in order to manage the project to a successful conclusion. Figure 18 shows TCPI (BAC) and TCPI (EAC) to show how upper and lower thresholds may be used to manage exceptions.

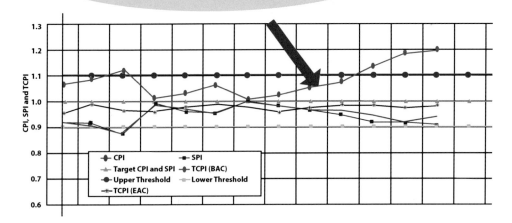

To Complete Performance Index for the Budget At Completion TCPI(BAC). The change in the level of efficiency needed to meet the milestone completion date as contracted.

Figure 18: Simple tests of reasonableness

Reproduced with kind permission from the APM Planning, Monitoring and Control Specific Interest Group working group

In Figure 19, the project manager has included the latest revised estimate (latest revised estimate (LRE) that has been included alongside the TCPI to achieve the work scope – or TC-BAC). You can see the differences between the TCPI for the budget at completion (BAC) (the blue line) as opposed to the LRE values indicated by the purple line.

It should be noted that as the LRE is directly related to the amount of remaining work. This may include changes to the scope, involving both increases and decreases, and draw-down of management reserve (MR) into the PMB.

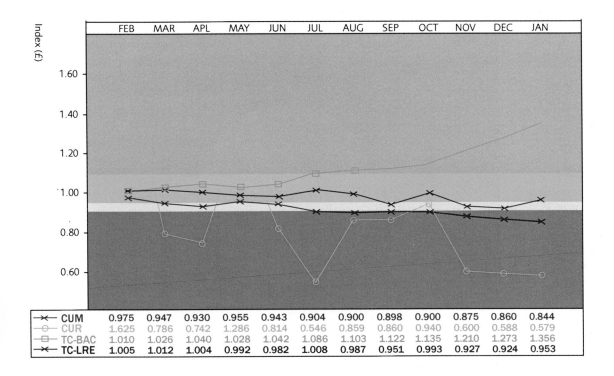

	FEB	MAR	APL	MAY	JUN	JUL	AUG	SEP	OCT	NOV	DEC	JAN
CUM	0.975	0.947	0.930	0.955	0.943	0.904	0.900	0.898	0.900	0.875	0.860	0.844
CUR	1.625	0.786	0.742	1.286	0.814	0.546	0.859	0.860	0.940	0.600	0.588	0.579
TC-BAC	1.010	1.026	1.040	1.028	1.042	1.086	1.103	1.122	1.135	1.210	1.273	1.356
TC-LRE	1.005	1.012	1.004	0.992	0.982	1.008	0.987	0.951	0.993	0.927	0.924	0.953

Figure 19: Tests of reasonableness for budget at completion (BAC) and latest revised estimate
Reproduced with kind permission from Deltek Inc and the APM Planning, Monitoring and Control Specific Interest Group working group

6.8 Producing reports derived from earned value measurements

Part of the EV analysis process is the production of a standard set of reports at the end of any period as part of the project performance review, for example, either a CAM review or a more senior management review. This can include graphs as well as tabulated data and some examples of both EV graphs and tabulated reports are shown below.

There is also a series of five standard reports that can be generated either manually or through an application, depending on project size and complexity. Examples of standard graphs include:

1. bulls-eye chart;
2. cost and schedule variance graphs;
3. tests of reasonableness;
4. milestone tracker or slippage charts;
5. independent estimate at completion (IEAC) curves.

The following benefits are realised when producing a report with the same periodic outputs:

- increased ease of trend analysis;
- decreased effort in producing information for management.

A management report does not need to include all graphical and tabulated data; it should include the information required by senior management to enable informed decision making.

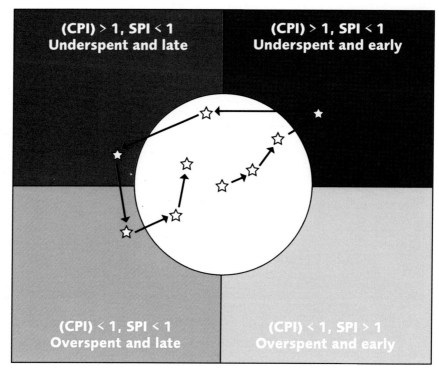

Cost performance index (CPI)

(CPI) > 1, SPI < 1
Underspent and late

(CPI) > 1, SPI < 1
Underspent and early

(CPI) < 1, SPI < 1
Overspent and late

(CPI) < 1, SPI > 1
Overspent and early

Schedule
performance index (SPI)

Figure 20: Bulls-eye chart
Taken from *Earned Value Management: APM Guidelines* (2008)

The bulls-eye chart does not show a trend as easily as a line graph can. It does however show the overall performance of the project or WBS element under consideration. Furthermore, the values are always from the current period and up to 10-12 reporting periods back. They therefore cannot be used in a predictive capacity. This particular chart also includes coloured sections that bind values of both CPI and SPI. It is up to an organisation if it uses a Red/Amber/Green (RAG) system. One advantage is that the project manager can see if CPI or SPI breaches a previously agreed tolerance. It also enables an indirect calculation to be made about the status of the project and possible changes to delivery dates and costs. For example, if the project has an overall SPI of 0.9 from the start, this means that for a project with a year's duration, the end date may be delayed by approximately five weeks.

Cost Performance Reports (CPRs) can be produced automatically by a number of software products. Some of the reports are tabulated, whilst others are graphical, though the same data is used. Each report represents different aspects of the same data for the reporting period in question:

- CPR1: project performance by WBS;
- CPR2: project performance by OBS;
- CPR3: baseline changes in the period;
- CPR4: resource profile (measured in either actual or equivalent people);
- CPR5: variance analysis.

CONTRACT PERFORMANCE REPORT : FORMAT 1 - WORK BREAKDOWN STRUCTURE

CONTRACTOR	2. CONTRACT	3. PROGRAM
NAME	a. NAME	a. NAME
LOCATION (Address and ZIP Code)	b. NUMBER	b. PHASE
		c. EVMS ACCEPTANCE
	c. TYPE	d. SHARE RATIO	NO

CONTRACT DATA

QUANTITY	b. NEGOTIATED COST	c. EST. COST AUTHORIZED UNPRICED WORK	d. TARGET PROFIT/ FEE	e. TARGET PRICE

ESTIMATED COST AT COMPLETION

	MANAGEMENT ESTIMATE AT COMPLETION (1)	CONTRACT BUDGET BASE (2)	VARIANCE (3)	a. NAME (Last, First, Middle Initial)
BEST CASE				
WORST CASE				
MOST LIKELY				

ITEM	CURRENT PERIOD					CUMULATIVE TO DATE	
	BUDGETED COST		ACTUAL COST WORK PERFORMED	VARIANCE		BUDGETED COST	
	WORK SCHEDULED	WORK PERFORMED		SCHEDULE	COST	WORK SCHEDULED	WORK PERFORMED
(1)	(2)	(3)	(4)	(5)	(6)	(7)	(8)
WORK BREAKDOWN STRUCTURE ELEMENT							
COST OF MONEY							
GENERAL & ADMINISTRATIVE							
UNDISTRIBUTED BUDGET							
SUBTOTAL (Performance Measurement Baseline)	0.00	0.00	0.00	0.00	0.00	0.00	0.00
MANAGEMENT RESERVE							
TOTAL	0.00	0.00	0.00	0.00	0.00	0.00	0.00
RECONCILIATION TO CONTRACT BUDGET BASE							
VARIANCE ADJUSTMENT							
TOTAL CONTRACT VARIANCE							

IN GBP _____

Form Approved

	4. REPORT PERIOD
	a. FROM *(YYYYMMDD)*
	b. TO *(YYYYMMDD)*

☐ **YES (YYYYMMDD)**

f. ESTIMATED PRICE	**g. CONTRACT CEILING**	**h. EST. CONTRACT CEILING**	**i. DATE OF OTB/OTS** *(YYYYMMDD)*

7. AUTHORIZED CONTRACTOR REPRESENTATIVE

	b. TITLE

c. SIGNATURE	**d. DATE SIGNED** *(YYYYMMDD*

ACTUAL	VARIANCE		REPROGRAMMING ADJUSTMENTS			AT COMPLETION		
COST WORK PERFORMED	SCHEDULE	COST	COST VARIANCE	SCHEDULE VARIANCE	BUDGET	BUDGETED	ESTIMATED	VARIANCE
(9)	(10)	(11)	(12a)	(12b)	(13)	(14)	(15)	(16)
0.00	0.00	0.00	0.00	0.00	0.00	0.00	0.00	0.00
0.00	0.00	0.00	0.00	0.00	0.00	0.00		
	0.00	0.00						

CPR1 should be used to determine project performance at a WP level at the end of the reporting period for which it has been been produced. If sufficient data has been captured in the WBS, it may be possible to produce a CPR1 report for activities and/or tasks within a WP.

Part of the EV analysis process is to perform a data check before performing any calculations and identifying results and options to keep the project on track.

It is important to:

- check all the values for both cumulative and periodic data add up to the values shown in the PMB;
- check that the cost and schedule variance values make sense;
- check to see that if actual costs and EV have been added, the BAC column is also non-zero;
- confirm that all combinations of ACWP, planned value (PV), EV and BAC contain zero values for both PPs;
- ensure that negative EV has not crept into the table since the last period. Do a quick calculation to find out what the cumulative EV (EV cum) is for the period and compare with the previous value;
- find out if the report has either been produced by a specific application or created by bespoke software.

The CPR2 report uses the same basic data, but it is produced through the OBS as opposed to the WBS. The same data checks should be made to ensure consistency. The CPR2 should be used to determine project performance at the end of the reporting period for which it has been produced. It may be possible to review performance within the supply chain OBS as well, if there is sufficient granularity.

CONTRACT PERFORMANCE REPORT : FORMAT 2 - ORGANISATIONAL CATEGORIES

CONTRACTOR	2. CONTRACT		3. PROGRAM
NAME	a. NAME		a. NAME
LOCATION (Address and ZIP Code)	b. NUMBER		b. PHASE
			c. EVMS ACCEPTANCE
	c. TYPE	d. SHARE RATIO	NO

PERFORMANCE DATA

ITEM (1)	CURRENT PERIOD					CUMULATIVE TO DATE	
	BUDGETED COST		ACTUAL COST WORK	VARIANCE		BUDGETED COST	
	WORK SCHEDULED	WORK PERFORMED		SCHEDULE	COST	WORK SCHEDULED	WORK PERFORMED
	(2)	(3)	(4)	(5)	(6)	(7)	(8)
ORGANIZATIONAL CATEGORY							
				0.00			
COST OF MONEY							
GENERAL & ADMINISTRATIVE							
UNDISTRIBUTED BUDGET							
SUBTOTAL (Performance Measurement Baseline)	0.00	0.00		0.00			
MANAGEMENT RESERVE							
TOTAL	0.00	0.00		0.00			

Table 14: Cost Performance Report No. 2
Reproduced with kind permission from Deltek Inc

IN GBP _____

Form Approved

4. REPORT PERIOD

a. FROM *(YYYYMMDD)*

b. TO *(YYYYMMDD)*

YES *(YYYYMMDD)*

	ACTUAL COST WORK	VARIANCE		REPROGRAMMING ADJUSTMENTS			AT COMPLETION		
		SCHEDULE	COST	COST VARIANCE	SCHEDULE VARIANCE	BUDGET	BUDGETED	ESTIMATED	VARIANCE
	(9)	(10)	(11)	(12a)	(12b)	(13)	(14)	(15)	(16)
0.00	0.00		0.00	0.00	0.00	0.00	0.00	0.00	0.0
0.00	0.00		0.00	0.00	0.00	0.00	0.00		

CONTRACTOR	2. CONTRACT	3. PROGRAM
NAME	a. NAME	a. NAME
LOCATION (Address and ZIP Code)	b. NUMBER	b. PHASE
		c. EVMS ACCEPTANCE
	c. TYPE	d. SHARE RATIO	NO

CONTRACT DATA

ORIGINAL NEGOTIATED COST	b. NEGOTIATED CONTRACT CHANGES	c. CURRENT NEGOTIATED COST (a. + b.) 0.00	d. ESTIMATED COST OF AUTHORIZED UNPRICED WORK
CONTRACT START DATE (YYYYMMDD)	i. CONTRACT DEFINITIZATION DATE (YYYYMMDD)	j. PLANNED COMPLETION DATE (YYYYMMDD)	k. CONTRACT COMPLETION DATE (YYYYMMDD)

PERFORMANCE DATA

ITEM	BCWS CUMULATIVE TO DATE	BCWS FOR REPORT PERIOD	BUDGETED COST FOR WORK SCHEDULED (BCWS) (Non-Cumulative)					
			SIX MONTH FORECAST (Enter names of months)					
			+1	+2	+3	+4	+5	+6
(1)	(2)	(3)	(4)	(5)	(5)	(7)	(8)	(9)
PERFORMANCE MEASUREMENT BASELINE (Beginning of Period)								
BASELINE CHANGES AUTHORIZED DURING REPORT PERIOD								
PERFORMANCE MEASUREMENT BASELINE (End of Period)								
MANAGEMENT RESERVE								
TOTAL								

Table 15: Cost Performance Report No. 3
Reproduced with kind permission from Deltek Inc

IN GBP _____

4. REPORT PERIOD

a. FROM (YYYYMMDD)

b. TO (YYYYMMDD)

☐ **YES** (YYYYMMDD)

e. CONTRACT BUDGET BASE (c. + d.) 0.00	f. TOTAL ALLOCATED BUDGET	g. DIFFERENCE (e. - f.) 0.00

I. ESTIMATED COMPLETION DATE (YYYYMMDD)

ENTER SPECIFIED PERIODS					UNDIS-TRIBUTED BUDGET	TOTAL BUDGET
(10)	(11)	(12)	(13)	(14)	(14)	(16)
						0
						0

The CPR3 report details any changes to the PMB, management reserve (MR) and the undistributed budget (UB) during the period. The EV practitioner can use this report along with the baseline change request (BCR) log to ensure that any change approved and implemented during the period has been reflected in the baseline. It can also be used to check if any unauthorised changes have been implemented in the baseline as well as being used to see if work has been moved without the correct amount of money or vice-versa. The CPR3 can also be used to check the PMB profile to verify if there are changes to this over successive reporting periods.

It is worth remembering and checking the following:
- if there is a difference between the beginning of the period and the end of the period values in the PMB for the period and in future periods;
- if some changes to the PMB have been made outside the six or 12 month window that is usually shown on this report – this can be checked by looking at the PMB profile across the entire project timeline and examining any changes between values from a window of successive periods, as shown in Figure 21;
- check and verify that the amounts shown in the CPR add up to those in the relevant change control requests. Check to see if money is being moved around without work or vice-versa;
- verify if there has been a request to draw-down money from the MR;
- verify that any amount requested from the MR, which has been moved into the PMB, add up to the remaining MR;
- verify if any changes have been made to the UB. As with the other change requests, check to ensure that the values add up;
- check that the UB is not being used to retrospectively modify previous performance.

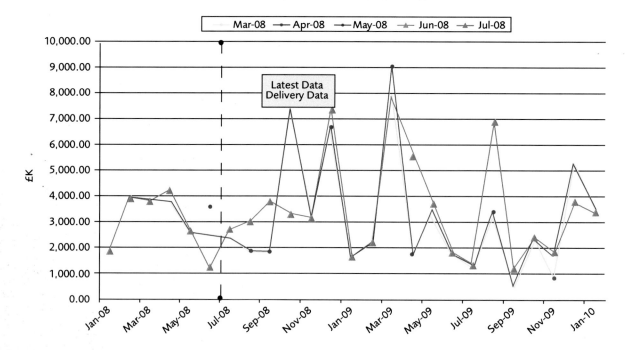

Figure 21: BCWS Baseline cross-check

Reproduced with kind permission from the APM Planning, Monitoring and Control Specific Interest Group working group

The CPR4 looks at the resource profile, usually using the OBS, for at least the next six months on the project. It can be used to check the following:

- that this profile has changed in line with change control requests;
- that any mix-ups between actual rates and full time equivalents have been identified;
- that any changes to the OBS that need to be included, are reflected in this report;
- to conduct simple tests of reasonableness – check to see if there are sufficient staff resources to complete the work scope from this point forward to the current scheduled end date. Cross refer to CPR2 and the relevant material allocation.

CONTRACT PERFORMANCE REPORT : FORMAT 4 - STAFFING

CONTRACTOR	2. CONTRACT	3. PROGRAM		
NAME	a. NAME	a. NAME		
LOCATION *(Address and ZIP Code)*	b. NUMBER	b. PHASE		
		c. EVMS ACCEPTANCE		
	c. TYPE	d. SHARE RATIO		NO

PERFORMANCE DATA *(All figures in whole numbers)*

ORGANIZATIONAL CATEGORY	ACTUAL CURRENT PERIOD	ACTUAL END OF CURRENT PERIOD (Cumulative)	FORECAST *(Non-Cumulative)*					
			SIX MONTH FORECAST BY MONTH *(Enter names of months)*					
			+1	+2	+3	+4	+5	
(1)	(2)	(3)	(4)	(5)	(6)	(7)	(8)	
TOTAL DIRECT	0	0	0	0	0	0	0	

Table 16: Cost Performance Report No. 4
Reproduced with kind permission from Deltek Inc

4. REPORT PERIOD

a. FROM *(YYYYMMDD)*

b. TO *(YYYYMMDD)*

YES *(YYYYMMDD)*

	ENTER SPECIFIED PERIODS					AT COMPLETION
+6						
(9)	(10)	(11)	(12)	(13)	(14)	(14)
0	0	0	0	0	0	0

CONTRACT PERFORMANCE REPORT : FORMAT 5 - VARIANCE ANALYSIS AND CORRECTIVE ACTIONS

CONTRACTOR	2. CONTRACT		3. PROGRAM	
NAME	a. NAME		a. NAME	
LOCATION *(Address and ZIP Code)*	b. NUMBER		b. PHASE	
			c. EVMS ACCEPTANCE	
	c. TYPE	d. SHARE RATIO		NO

EVALUATION

Discussion should include but is not limited to:

Summary Analysis:
Summary of Overall Contract Variances
Differences between EAC's (Blocks 6.a., 6.b., 6.c., or Block 8.15)
Changes in Undistributed Budget
Changes in Management Reserve
Significant timephasing shifts in Baseline (BCWS) (Format 3)
Significant timephasing shifts or overall changes in Forecasted Staffing (Format 4)
Discussion of Over Target Baseline and/or Over Target Schedule incorporation

Analysis of Significant Variances (identify and describe each):
Type and Magnitude of Variance
Explanation of Significant Reasons
Effect on Immediate Task
Effect on Total Contract
Corrective Actions Taken or Planned

Table 17: Cost Performance Report No. 5
Reproduced with kind permission from Deltek Inc

4. REPORT PERIOD

a. FROM *(YYYYMMDD)*

b. TO *(YYYYMMDD)*

YES *(YYYYMMDD)*

The CPR5 is produced when either a cost or schedule variance has exceeded an agreed threshold for a specific WP or CA. For example, a schedule variance in excess of +-10% would trigger a CPR5 report for the relevant WP. The CAM responsible for that specific WP would need to provide an explanation for the variance and explain what action is being, or will be taken to ensure performance improves.

Check that the explanations make sense. Are there explanations that relate to cost variance that should be in the schedule variance section (or vice versa)?

Check that the corrective action proposed returns performance to a more favourable cost variance (CV) or schedule variance (SV). If so, confirm whether this is either a returns performance to a specified threshold or a return to zero.

These reports are normally used on projects where producing them manually would take too much time and effort. Manual analysis of the data would also prove costly for the same reason. As a result, they are usually produced by a commercial software application and used on projects with relatively large budgets, where parts of the work scope are performed by partners or sub-contractors.

Small projects and project managers on fast-moving or short projects may not need such software and reporting systems to answer their customer's or client's questions. In this case, the project manager may scale and/or tailor the CPR to a much smaller set of reports or remove them altogether.

6.9 Defining appropriate variance thresholds

6.9.1 Why should variance thresholds be set?

Cost and variance thresholds should be set because:

- they trigger the production of a CPR5 from the relevant CAM along with details of the corrective action(s);
- they contribute to project trends analysis for either the entire project or a specific phase or stage;
- they provide information to support the change management process;
- they provide one of the early warning mechanisms that inform the project manager if and when corrective action should be taken;
- where possible, they should be based on previous performance norms, on LFE data and modified to fit within the project's context.

6.9.2 When should variance thresholds be set?

Thresholds should be set before the project schedule is baselined and should relate only to the current project phase or stage, as a variance threshold for similar work types may be different in other phases or stages.

The threshold for the CA or WP should be based on the following:

- the total amount of money allocated;
- the cost profile;
- the EVT used;
- if materials are being purchased, the need and chance of accruals;
- whether the work package is part of a supply chain, and performance data is being aggregated – will the variance be magnified or diminished as a result?
- the amount of MR allocated;
- the amount of risk mitigation allocated;
- whether the threshold needs to have a single or double trigger (for example >10%, or <10% or a combination of two).

The CAM should also consider if the threshold will be affected by being measured as a relative (periodic) or absolute (cumulative) measurement.

6.9.3 When should thresholds change and why?

Variance threshold values should be changed if it is found that:

- the threshold is either continually or rarely triggered, even when the variance has significant impacts on other WPs;
- the project phase, stage or WP is nearing completion and the variance is becoming negligible when compared with the cumulative values of BCWP and ACWP.

6.10 Calculating estimates at completion and their application

EVM can be used as a predictor of project output in terms of the final cost of the project. This is called an estimate at completion (EAC). There are many formulae that use past performance, CPI, SPI or both, as indicators of future performance, and hence calculate an EAC. Because we use formulae, the EAC is called an independent EAC (IEAC), i.e. there is no judgement on the part of CAMs or project manager.

Examples of these IEACs are as follows:

IEAC = ACWP + ((BAC − BCWP) / (CPI x SPI))
IEAC = BAC/CPI
IEAC = ACWP + ((BAC − BCWP) / ((CPI x 0.8) x (SPI x 0.2)))

However, using past performance to predict future outcomes may not be the best way of determining a project's EAC. CAMs and project managers may have more information on the project's EAC based on influencing factors on the remaining work. This would be a more subjective view of the EAC.

When declaring a project's EAC, the project manager will have to take a balanced view by comparing the IEAC and the subjective EAC. If the EAC lies between the resultant IEAC calculations, then the project manager can gain confidence that it may be a reasonable estimate. To test whether a subjective EAC is reasonable, the project manager can apply a test by using the to complete performance indicator (TCPI) formula:

$TCPI_{EAC}$ = (BAC − BCWP) / (EAC − ACWP)
This divides the remaining work, (numerator), by the amount of resources that are needed to meet the subjective EAC (denominator).

A value greater than 1.0 will indicate to the project manager that the project will have to perform more cost efficiently than it has in the past if the subjective EAC is to be reached. A $TCPI_{EAC}$ of 1.1 informs the project manager that the project will have to perform 10% more efficiently on the remaining work if it is going to reach the subjective EAC, therefore the EAC is likely to be understated and needs revising upwards.

The project manager can also use the CPI to assist in their decision making process. As a rule of thumb, a project that has consistently been overspent, indicated by a CPI of less than 1.0, and a $TCPI_{EAC}$ of greater than 1.1, is unlikely to suddenly improve its cost efficiency in the future. This suggests the EAC is insufficient, although every case will have to be examined on its own merits.

There is another TCPI formula, which is:

$$TCPI_{BAC} = (BAC - BCWP) / (BAC - ACWP)$$

This divides the remaining work, (numerator), by the amount of resources that are needed to meet the BAC (denominator).

This formula relates to how realistic the budget is. Again, if the $TCPI_{BAC}$ is 1.1, this informs the project manager that the project will have to perform 10% more efficiently on the remaining work if it is going to meet the BAC.

No one indicator will provide enough information for the project manager to make informed decisions. It is important for the project manager to observe trends, manage by exception using thresholds and use all the information that an EVMS can generate in order to manage the project to a successful conclusion.

6.11 Calculating and interpreting tests of reasonableness and independent estimates at completion

In producing these, it should be noted that there are two different types of EAC, the one that is automatically calculated, and the one generated by using the project manager's (or CAM's) estimate. Both are equally valid calculations. However, it should be noted that the only difference between the calculations is the estimated amount of remaining work.

6.12 Interpreting earned value data to identify likely causes of reported performance

Thresholds are used to identify if the cost/time variances and indices are moving towards a trigger point. These threshold points should be agreed at the start of the project with the steering board. If these need to change over time, it is important to record these changes, and ensure that reporting systems, graphs etc. are updated at the relevant point.

An EV practitioner needs to use data generated by the EVMS or project control system description to understand the variances and trends that are produced. In addition, the EV practitioner needs to be able to understand the likely causes and potential effects of the reported performance. By analysing these likely causes, an EV practitioner will be able to identify the corrective action required and the implications of each action. This is covered in section 6.13 on page 111.

Inputs

- Verified EV data up to and including the latest reporting period.
- An agreed set of IEAC calculations for use in the trend analysis.
- The latest updated version of the schedule.
- The latest set of change requests to be submitted for approval.
- The current values for the PMB and MR and their profiles.
- The latest edition of the project risk, issues and opportunities registers, if separated out.
- The latest set of CPRs – 1 to 5 inclusive.
- The latest version of a milestone progress chart. There is bespoke or commercially available software to drill-down the performance data for each WBS level in the project.

Methods

- Use the latest EV data to produce the CPI, SPI, SV, CV, TCPI and IEAC values.
- Plot the values generated above in a graphical form that shows all IEAC values with the BAC (and EAC if appropriate) and ensure the BAC value is also included for comparison.
- Reconcile values for the remaining work with the schedule.

- Update the milestone progress chart where applicable.
- Plot the latest PMB profile alongside previous versions and identify any uncontrolled changes.
- Update the project risk network/schedule and perform cost/schedule risk analysis (SRA).
- Review the EV time/cost performance trends against the confidence limits produced from the risk analysis for a major milestone or event.
- Check that the values for the MR and PMB have been reconciled with the contract budget baseline (CBB).

Considerations:

- Use a linear graph instead of a bulls-eye or quad chart, so that both the time and cost related trends for the project are visible.
- If there are any uncontrolled changes in the PMB, check to see where these are within the WBS by drilling-down.
- If the MR and PMB do not reconcile with the current CBB, establish which value has changed. Has work been moved without the relevant budget being moved with it, or vice versa?
- Identify whether any MR has been drawn down without authority. Does the new value still reconcile with the CBB and PMB? If not then either the reserve or the PMB has altered. Check the cost performance report No.3 to find out how many authorised changes have been made in the last period.
- Identify whether any MR is being used to mask either cost or schedule variances.
- Check if the schedule changes have introduced negative lags, 'hard' constraints, recurring or recursive logic.
- Look at the critical path and the amount of float on activities within the WBS. Check to see if the amount of float has changed drastically within a period, or if the float has steadily increased or decreased over time. It is also advisable to check and see the overall distribution of activity/task float across the project, for example, float critical/supercritical/1-10 days.

Historical data checks

- Check that the PMB and MR add up to the CBB. If they are different, look into the reasons for this discrepancy. Check to see if the BAC changed and to what extent.
- Check to find out if work has been moved with or without budget.
- Check to see if the PMB profile has changed. Challenge any changes that have not been made through the project's CPP.
- Verify whether any MR has been drawn down. Verify that the new value still reconciles with the CBB and PMB.
- Check whether any actual costs been incorrectly recorded or attributed.
- Verify any changes that have been made to the PMB within the period.
- Check Performance trends within WPs and the whole project. Identify if there are any unexplained peaks troughs
- Identify whether any risks have impacted within the period. Review the s-curves for the cost and schedule in order to establish the impact and where fallback action must be inserted into the plan.
- Critical path and amount and type of float (for example critical/supercritical/1-10 days, etc.) How has the activity spread within the schedule?
- Schedule adherence – check and verify to find any WPs being started ahead of their scheduled start date.
- Check to see if PPs are being turned into WPs ahead of the date defined by the rolling wave lead time.
- Are there changing EV techniques in a period?
- Is there use of negative lag in one or more periods?
- Is incorrect EV data being used, either accidentally or unknowingly?
- Identify whether MR is being used to mask variances.
- Establish if any artificial constraints have been added in during a period that acts as a brick wall for a part of the project.
- The project manager may wish to use the many milestones approach. For example, if there are five activities within a WP, each one is assigned an amount of the total WP budget or it can be assumed that each activity will have the same value (20% in this case). The value or progress is claimed/earned as each activity is verified as complete.

Forecast data checks

- Milestone delivery trends.
- IEAC trends.
- To complete performance index (TCPI) for costs.
- Convergence on a known milestone date – is it happening?
- Comparison of probable 10/50/90 data with EV data – are they trending/converging at similar rates?

Interpretation

Agreed thresholds should be used to identify whether the cost/time variances and indices are moving towards a trigger point. These thresholds should be agreed at the start of the project with the steering board. If these need to change over time, it is important to record these changes and ensure that reporting systems, graphs, etc. are updated at the relevant point.

The EV practitioner is looking for trends in IEAC, variance and performance indices. The IEAC is important as an estimate as it provides an indication of future completion costs assuming that current performance does not change. The EV practitioner should look at the range of IEAC values and the rate of convergence, if it has reduced very quickly and remains reduced, then this may indicate that a severe cost control has been imposed on the project. It may also indicate that progress has been made ahead of schedule. In the latter case, check that corners have not been cut in claiming this progress. This can be cross-checked with the EV data for any changes in EV type during a specific period, as well checking if progress has been claimed when none shouldhave been. By comparing and contrasting the schedule trend data (for example, the milestone trend chart) with the cost data, it can be established that if milestone dates are not converging and getting later, then it is highly likely that there is very tight control over the budget and this will in turn affect the schedule.

Confidence limits from risk data should be compared with the EV data to identify any trends and convergence at similar rates towards the same milestone or event. This may help establish if one or more project risks have occurred.

It is important to check for any WP values that creep up (game playing). For instance, 92% and 93% complete in successive periods. There are ways of mitigating this, for example, when a WP is 90% or 95% complete (this has to be agreed with stakeholders beforehand) the EV is no longer used as a progress measure. Start using measures that relate to the number of snags/issues/checks that have been completed. Look for acceptance, handover and closeout, rather than pure EV as the measures for success. These could be planned as activities in their own right.

Checks should be made to identify whether WPs are being started ahead of their scheduled start date and if they are being started out of schedule sequence. In addition, verify if any PPs have actual costs being accrued without being turned into WPs. Lastly, check that PPs are not being turned into WPs ahead of the date defined by the rolling wave planning process.

Outputs

Following these reviews and checks the following should be updated:
- IEAC graphs;
- MR and PMB values, where necessary;
- change control requests;
- the risk register;
- the milestone progress chart;
- cost and schedule risk analysis.

6.13 Selecting appropriate courses of action based on earned value data

The analysis from the variance thresholds process (section 6.9 on page 106) provides options for courses of action that may be used to amend the PMB through the project's change control process (CCP). The change will introduce a recovery plan that will do one of two things:

1. change the PMB so that the original project objectives can still be met;
2. change the PMB so that the objectives can be met, but within an altered budget and timescale.

Each option will have a different impact on the PMB and the EV practitioner will need to articulate these clearly to ensure the project manager and project stakeholders understand the implications of approving a specific change.

Inputs

- IEAC graphs;
- MR and PMB values, where necessary;
- change control requests;
- the risk register;
- the milestone progress chart;
- cost and schedule risk analysis;
- Current EV data, SPI, CPI, TCPI and BAC values.

Methods

From the data provided, establish if the issue is with cost, time or both of these elements. Check to see if the cause is either a cost or time overrun or underrun and establish if the MR for time and cost is being consumed at a higher rate than expected.

The main question to ask is what action needs to be taken to recover. Recovery in this instance means to ensure that the project performance returns to an agreed level (for example the CV and SV return to zero) and that the delivery forecasts for time and cost return to those detailed in the contract. In some cases, recovery to zero variance may not be possible. It may, however be possible to recover to green. In this instance, green is a term related to the threshold bands set for the cost and schedule variances and indices. For example, the values for green, amber and red for both CPI and SPI may be set as:
Green >=1.1<=CPI >= to 0.95
Amber 0.9 >= CPI < 0.95
Red <0.9

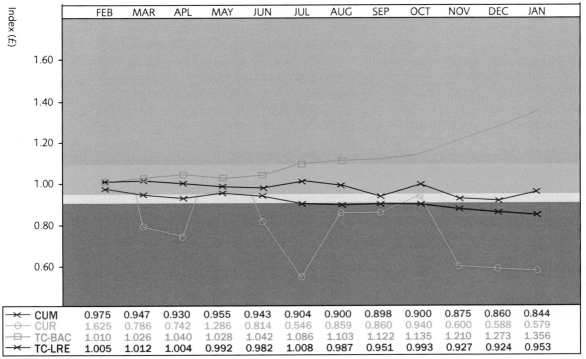

	FEB	MAR	APL	MAY	JUN	JUL	AUG	SEP	OCT	NOV	DEC	JAN
CUM	0.975	0.947	0.930	0.955	0.943	0.904	0.900	0.898	0.900	0.875	0.860	0.844
CUR	1.625	0.786	0.742	1.286	0.814	0.546	0.859	0.860	0.940	0.600	0.588	0.579
TC-BAC	1.010	1.026	1.040	1.028	1.042	1.086	1.103	1.122	1.135	1.210	1.273	1.356
TC-LRE	1.005	1.012	1.004	0.992	0.982	1.008	0.987	0.951	0.993	0.927	0.924	0.953

This is illustrated in Figure 22.

Figure 22: TCPI BAC graph showing red, amber and green performance thresholds
Reproduced with kind permission from Deltek Inc and the APM Planning, Monitoring and Control Specific Interest Group
working group

To select the most appropriate course of action, it is recommended that the following process be used:

- use the SPI, CPI and TCPI values to establish whether any changes can be made and if these changes can be made within project scope or if the PMB requires external change. It may be possible to change the work scope of one or more CAs without affecting the overall project scope. The TCPI value will indicate the change in efficiency required to recover from the current position;
- use the following options to change the work scope, assuming that the project is not itself being stopped or delayed:
- start a WP, activity or PP;
- stop and remove a WP, activity or PP from the work scope. Check to see how this changes the project objectives or requirements within the business case;
- accelerate a WP, activity or PP;
- delay a WP, activity or PP;
- alter the resources allocated to a WP, task or activity;
- change the project assumptions. In doing this, check that any changes to the RBS are captured and assess any new risks that may arise;
- change the resources or resource profile for an activity, WP or entire phase;
- change one or more of the project's requirements. This will need agreement from the project sponsor and steering board;
- check the financial and commercial positions, especially for milestone payment, cash flow and net present value where

appropriate;
- check that key resources are available when required;
- assess the potential impact on any sub-contracts should the change be accepted and implemented;
- check the amount of float on activities to ensure the critical milestones and events have not changed;
- check that the critical path, if different, is reflected in the risk network or schedule;
- follow the risk management process in the risk management section on page 119 to update the cost and schedule risk analysis;
- update the OBS and RAM to ensure that no allocation conflicts occur and reconcile the amounts of DB, UB and MR, where MR has been moved into DB.

These should be repeated until a new work scope has been generated. Approval should be sought through the normal change control route before changes can be implemented.

Outputs

Following these reviews and checks the following should be updated:
- the WBS and RAM;
- the cost and schedule risk analysis;
- the schedule;
- the cash flow profile;
- the resource profile.

In the event that no option can be found that enables the project to 'return to zero', then the same process should be used to provide a series of options that show the changes to the work scope as well as the changes to the time and cost to deliver that remaining work scope. For example, if recovery is set to 'green' this may mean no better than 0.95. In schedule terms, this could mean that if the project had another 12 months of remaining work before completion, it would be over two weeks late.

7 Change management

7.1 The definition and purpose of management reserve

Management reserve (MR) is an amount of the total allocated budget withheld for management control purposes rather than designated for the achievement of a specific task or set of tasks. It is not a part of the performance measurement baseline.

Baselines are updated by adding extra budget for additional work scope and/or transferring MR into the budget baseline. The MR budget can be transferred only with management approval and all transfers should be documented and authorised. Please refer to the Planning section 4.10 and Change management section 7.4 on pages 60 and 115 respectively.

MR is a portion of the contract budget baseline (CBB) It is held separately for future allocation to CAs and will be used, if required, to cover increased work scope requirements resulting from unforeseen changes that fall within the overall scope of the contract.

The MR must never be used to eliminate past or current cost or schedule variances. This does not prevent the allocation of reserve to future efforts in problem areas if the project manager agrees there is due cause.

Where changes in work scope are requested by the customer, MR should not be used. Such changes are covered by contract amendments with agreed prices. The CBB is then increased to reflect the changes in work scope and budget.

7.2 The definition and purpose of an audit trail

An audit trail is a sequence of steps supported by evidence documenting the real processing of a transaction flow through an organisation, a process or a system.

An audit log is a chronological sequence of audit records, each of which contains evidence directly relating to, and resulting from, the execution of a business process or system function.

The change management process ensures any change is assessed and incorporated into the project baseline in a timely and controlled manner. It ensures that the project formally maintains the integrity of both the CBB and the PMB. It is important that all changes to past, present and future information are embodied in the PMB in an orderly and documented manner. This enables it to remain an accurate representation of all authorised work.

7.3 Typical sources of baseline change requests

Change requests can come from different sources, but typically come from three areas:

1. customer;
2. project manager;
3. CAM.

7.4 When baseline change is appropriate or inappropriate

There are three types of baseline change:

1. baseline maintenance (including rolling wave planning);
2. re-planning;
3. re-baselining.

7.4.1 Baseline maintenance

There are changes that do not change the integrity of the PMB, which can be:

- The conversion of PPs to WPs where the planning structure is the same;
- opening and closing WPs;
- changes to descriptive information, e.g. control account title.

A baseline change is not needed for the regular forecast plan updates; these are merely part of the normal update process that should be followed by the project team.

7.4.2 Re-planning

Re-planning constitutes a change to the PMB within the budget and timescale constraints of the existing CBB. Re-planning can be a consequence of either internal or customer-requested change.

Internal re-planning should only be used when, according to current performance, areas of the forecast plan cannot be realistically recovered which in turn would cause a failure to meet contractual objectives. Re-planning should not be used to cover legitimate cost and/or schedule variances.

7.4.2.1 Rules for re-planning

Customer requested change
Where contract out of scope work is requested, a re-plan may be conducted to incorporate this into the PMB. This should follow the normal baseline change process and should be fully auditable. This could affect the project objectives and may result in an amended budget and timescale, which in turn would result in a new PMB.

If there is a compelling requirement from the customer for a contract change to be made urgently prior to its negotiation and approval, then the customer and project manager may agree to proceed with this as authorised un-priced work (AUW). To allow for this, budget should be released by the project manager from the MR and placed into the UB. This will then be distributed as new work scope to the CAM(s). The project manager will then instruct the CAM(s) to raise a baseline change request to formally incorporate the AUW into their cost account plan (CAP). The change request should then be progressed in the normal manner.

Authorised un-priced work will be incorporated into the PMB by increasing the project target cost by the amount estimated for that work using UB as the holding account. In order to mitigate any risk, a limit of liability should be agreed with the customer prior to allocating the temporary internal budget. Where budget exceeds the limit of liability, the project target cost will only increase if both parties agree to this.

Following formal negotiation and approval, the project target cost will be adjusted to reflect the final negotiated contract change. On receipt of a formal contract amendment from the customer, the MR is credited with the original estimated value that had been placed into the UB. Any difference between this original estimate and the final negotiated change should be reconciled using MR. The UB is unaffected by the receipt of the negotiated change.

Concise records of all budget changes should be maintained to ensure reconciliation to the original assigned budgets.

Organisational change
Only under exceptional circumstances, for example where a new CAM has been appointed and the current PMB is deemed unworkable, may the new CAM request a re-plan. Where current variances exist, a re-plan cannot be applied just to allow a new CAM to start with a clean sheet. Under such circumstances, a re-plan should be justified and approved by a wider project change forum.

Work and budget transfer between control accounts
When contract in scope work is transferred between CAs, this invokes a re-plan. Work transfer should be accompanied with the associated budget and be agreed by all affected parties.

Work and budget transfer within a control account
Where clear evidence exists establishing that work scope has been incorrectly assigned within a CA between resource code, calendar years and WPs, a re-plan may be requested within the confines of the existing CA schedule and budget. Such changes should not be used to cover legitimate variances.

Significant change in resource availability
Where a significant change exists in organisational resource availability, resulting in idle resources or the inability to complete WPs, a re-plan may be requested at the discretion of the project manager.

Re-work
Unplanned re-work may initiate a re-plan in order to create new WPs to perform that work. Under these circumstances, the budget should be assigned from MR.

Change to earned value type
Where clear evidence exists to verify that the EV type has been incorrectly assigned to a WP, a re-plan may be requested.

Change to work packages as part of rolling wave planning
As more detail of the work content becomes available, the PP can be converted to a WP. A re-plan may be requested for schedule and budget change. In such instances, any change in budget should be reconciled with MR or UB accordingly.

Do not:
- transfer work scope or budget independently of one another;
- make retrospective changes to previously reported actual costs except for accounting adjustments and corrections of errors;
- transfer unused budget from closed WPs to other WPs or PPs;
- add additional budget to WPs that are already open unless otherwise approved by the project manager.

Baselines are updated by adding extra budget for the additional work scope and/or transferring contingency budget (the MR) into the budget baseline. MR can only be transferred with the project manager's approval and all transfers should be fully documented and authorised.

The additional budget can be incorporated into the project using these approaches:

- new WPs can be generated solely for the budget transferred;
- existing WPs can be closed and new WPs opened to include outstanding work, plus the additional budget.

It is important to note that additional budget should not be assigned to a closed WP.

When the new baseline has been completed, the overall future budget graph should be re-calculated and a new graph produced from the current date until completion. This will result in a saw-tooth graph. The project budget and performance graphs should not be re-calculated back to day one of the project.

7.4.3 Re-programme (or re-baselining)

A re-programme is the re-planning of the remaining contractual effort that results in a revised total allocated budget and/or schedule which will exceed, or fall short of, the current contract budget base (CBB). This may require customer approval.

Formal re-programming may be allowed when performance measurement against the contract budget base becomes unworkable due to overruns in cost and/or schedule. This will result in an Over Target Baseline (OTB) and/or Over Schedule Baseline (OSB) in order to monitor, report and control the remaining work:

- **Over Target Baseline** is the re-planning of the remaining effort in the contract, resulting in a new budget allocation which exceeds the CBB;
- **Over Schedule Baseline** is the re-planning of the remaining effort in the contract, resulting in the programme schedule exceeding the contractual dates but remaining within the existing budget.

Formal re-programming requires prior knowledge, analysis (including comprehensive EAC) and approval from the customer. Upon formal approval, re-programming may result in a change to the existing PMB and identification of additional budget for new work that may not have been previously planned.

There are three options available with an OTB or OSB:

1. all variances can be eliminated by setting both the BCWS and BCWP equal to the ACWP;
2. schedule variance can be eliminated by setting the BCWS equal to BCWP;
3. maintain variances to date.

7.4.3.1 Rules of re-programming (as re-planning plus)

There must be formal, documented customer authorisation to implement the OTB/OSB plan and there should be a minimum of six months' contract work remaining.

Key activities in change management
- Identify and raise necessary changes to the CA.
- Integrate, where applicable, change to associated risks.
- Ensure that all changes to the PMB are reflected within the associated forecast plans.
- Ensure that changes are embodied within all elements of the management system (for example the toolset, documentation, reports, etc.).

7.5 Appropriate and inappropriate uses of management reserve

Management reserve (MR) must never be used to eliminate past or present cost or schedule variances. This does not prevent the allocation of reserve for future efforts in problem areas, if the project manager agrees there is due cause.

A project's MR should not be used for changes in work scope originating from the customer. These are covered by contract amendments with agreed prices. The CBB is then increased to reflect the changes in work scope and budget.

Baselines are updated by adding extra budget for additional work scope and/or transferring MR into the budget baseline. The MR budget can be transferred only with management approval and all transfers should be documented and authorised. The additional budgets can be incorporated into the project as follows:

new WPs can be generated solely for the budget transferred;
existing WPs can be closed and new WPs opened to include the outstanding work, plus the additional budget.

Additional budget should not be assigned to a closed WP. If the current baseline is being amended, history should not be changed. The focus should be on establishing a workable plan for the accomplishment of the remaining efforts.

Please refer to Planning section 4.10 and Change management section 7.4 on pages 60 and 115 respectively for more information on the inappropriate use of MR.

7.6 The impact of changing baselines

The approved project baseline is the time-phased budget against which both project progress and performance are measured and reported. This baseline is used as the budgeted cost of work scheduled.

A baseline plan defines not only the financial baseline and structures for a project but also the timescales, resources and boundaries of the plan.

Changes to the current baseline must be strictly controlled in order to maintain a valid basis for the project performance assessment. The current baseline must be traceable back to the original baseline, and be reconcilable to the current authorised scope, schedule and cost objectives.

7.7 Defining and implementing a robust process for the authorisation and management of baseline change

Authorised changes should be incorporated in a timely manner, recording the effects of such changes in budgets and schedules.

Retrospective changes to records relating to work performed should be tightly controlled due to the risk of those changes affecting previously reported amounts for actual costs, EV or budgets. Adjustments should only ever be made for the correction of errors, routine accounting adjustments, effects of customer or management directed changes or to improve baseline integrity and accuracy of performance measurement data.

Revisions to the project budget, except for authorised changes, should be prevented and all changes to the PMB well documented. Changes must be formally requested by the CAM via a baseline change request (BCR) and should be approved by the change board before they can be implemented.

8 Risk management

8.1 The benefits of risk assessment

Project risk analysis and management is a process which enables the analysis and management of the risks associated with a project. Properly undertaken it will increase the likelihood of successful completion of a project to cost, time and performance objectives. It should be regarded as an integral part of project or business management and not just as a set of tools or techniques.

The integration of EVM and risk management should provide more realistic earned value assessments and give a better estimate of the project completion cost and timescale.

The benefits of systematic risk identification and risk management (RM) include:

- more realistic business and project planning;
- actions being implemented in time to be effective;
- greater certainty of achieving business goals and project objectives;
- appreciation of, and readiness to exploit, all beneficial opportunities;
- improved loss control;
- improved control of project and business costs;
- increased flexibility as a result of understanding all options and their associated risks;
- greater control over innovation and business development;
- fewer costly surprises through effective and transparent contingency planning.

8.2 How and where risk management can be integrated with earned value management

Earned value management and risk management are complementary processes. Both are key aspects of the overall project management discipline. Risk management is largely related to what may happen in the future; earned value management is concerned with using what has already happened to predict and control the future. There may be great synergies to be realised by integrating the two processes.

The following list suggests areas where risk management may be usefully integrated with earned value management:

- estimating the project activities (cost and schedule):
  - project activities;
  - risk mitigation activities;
  - contingency activities;
- establishing management reserve budget;
- creating and controlling the budget and schedule for the RM process – i.e. those elements of the overall project management activities that cover risk management (not to be confused with the MR budget);
- scheduling:
  - incorporating RM activities in the baseline schedule;
  - establishing dependencies;
  - determining risk inherent within the schedule by using statistical risk network analysis;
  - risk modelling to optimise project schedules;

- including RM activities in project performance analysis:
  - including resource, cost and schedule for risk management activities in overall project earned value;
  - using earned value to determine the performance of the risk management activities, e.g. identifying if the mitigation plan is likely to be achieved on time and to budget;
- development of forecasts:
  - estimate at completion (cost);
  - schedule forecast (time);
  - modelling with the risk network;
- change management: incorporation of MR budget for contingency activities.

If the EVM system has been established in accordance with this guide, then the key integrating structures will have been defined, namely the work breakdown structure and the project schedule/network. These structures are ideal for storing and defining information about the project and would therefore provide logical and convenient structures for risk reporting. Each element in the structure contains the data that is commonly used to inform quantitative risk analysis and would also provide a convenient place for noting qualitative risks at the point where they are likely to occur. Further, if the structure defines the whole project then a complete risk checklist can be stored and compiled with no danger of oversight.

In 2008 APM published further guidance, *Interfacing Risk and Earned Value Management*.

This takes the approach that the key to EVM and RM interfacing lies in the recognition that added value can be found in both disciplines through commonality of purpose in setting, measuring and achieving project targets. A baseline that takes no account of risk is extremely unlikely to be achieved; similarly, risk response actions that are not resourced and effectively monitored are unlikely to produce the desired results.

The guide has set out to establish the principles and potential practices for a closer relationship between the EVM and RM disciplines. These principles can be used to develop and inform the advancement of organisations' RM and EVM capability.

8.3 Using risk management approaches in setting the performance measurement baseline

The project contract budget baseline consists of the performance measurement baseline (PMB) and the amount of management reserve (MR) calculated and agreed for the project. The MR is generated after agreeing the risk appetite, and the exposure and tolerance for the project.

The following points should be used in generating the risk appetite:

- develop the WBS and schedule without a hidden contingency or buffer;
- allocate costs and resources in the schedule. These costs should be deterministic or single-point at this stage;
- assess the estimating uncertainty with 3-point estimates for time and cost. Some organisations will have standard estimating tolerances for project phases, project types and specific activities. These should be used to locate deterministic or single-point values within upper and lower tolerances. In some instances, estimates for specific tasks and activities can be taken from data sources from within the company or organisation. In addition, some industrial sectors and industries have estimating manuals and/or databases. If these are used, consideration should be made to create a 3-point estimate from a single value, using the tolerances mentioned above;
- review and agree the estimates and document the values;

- where appropriate, a risk schedule should be created from the master schedule. This should be approximately 200-300 tasks, activities and milestones. These activities, tasks and milestones should be chosen by considering those activities that are on or very near the critical path, those that are significant or relevant (these should be defined) to the project. Too many tasks and the risk schedule becomes insensitive to any changes following updates to the schedule; it also results in very small changes to the confidence limits and therefore the risk appetite, as the project progresses. Too few activities may result in costs and tasks being over-aggregated and result in a jagged s-curve. The output it may be too sensitive to changes and may be difficult to pick a specific output;
- combine and reconcile task and activity times and costs for those activities that have been removed from the master schedule;
- ensure the risk schedule is in a sufficiently mature state to conduct cost and schedule risk analysis (CRA/SRA). This can be performed either manually or by using software applications;
- conduct the SRA/CRA;
- communicate the result to stakeholders and agree the cost and schedule limit;

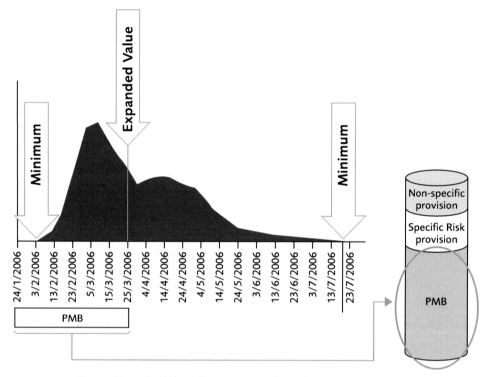

Figure 23: Schedule risk analysis to help determine the PMB
Taken from *Interfacing Risk and Earned Value Management* (APM, 2008)

- the overall cost and schedule should be reconciled back into activities in the risk schedule and from there to the master schedule;
- the cost and schedule exposure as shown in figure 23 should not be discarded. Consideration should be given to retaining some of the task or activity uncertainty as part of the MR. Care should be taken to avoid the double accounting of cost and schedule reserve when conducting CRA/SRA. In addition, any of the uncertainty exposure that is moved into the MR and is allocated to significant, relevant or critical activities/tasks should be documented along with a justification for this.

The next stage of the process requires the addition of risks to the risk schedule. This relies on the project already having a documented set of assumptions.

8.4 Using risk management approaches to establish the level of management reserve for specific and non-specific risks

It is important to know how to calculate the amount of management reserve (MR) for the project. The previous section dealt with how to use risk management approaches to set the PMB. This section adds to this by using a similar process to calculate the amount of MR and the total risk appetite for the project. The MR should be as robust as possible and should consist of both the cost and schedule reserve for both specific and non-specific risks.

Inputs

- The latest PMB, created using risk management methods.
- The amount of agreed buffer resulting from the risk management method used.
- The latest risk register, including a list of agreed mitigation actions.
- The latest issue of the project schedule.
- Bespoke or commercially available risk analysis software to conduct the cost and schedule risk analysis (CRA/SRA).
- The learning from experience (LFE) database from previous similar projects.

Methods

- Assumptions should be reviewed to establish a link to an existing risk, or a new risk should be raised if required. Update the risk register using the agreed risk management process.
- Identify the risks and establish risk mitigation actions and a fallback plan. Start to plan the mitigation and fallback actions and ensure that the fallback control actions are included with the mitigation plans.
- Prioritise the risks, including the mitigation and fallback plans. Identify this in the audit trail and risk register.
- Conduct a cost/benefits analysis of the mitigation actions to ensure they are financially viable and worth committing to. It is suggested that if a return on investment process is employed to help in the cost-benefit analysis, that any return on investment calculation used is consistently applied to all mitigation plans.
- Map the Risk Mitigation Action (RMA) into activities and/or tasks in the master schedule. Ensure an audit trail is used to link these together. These must be reconciled into the risk schedule, for example as part of an overall activity or a stand-alone activity/task. Care must be taken to ensure that double accounting has not taken place.
- Where necessary, reconcile the risk fallback (post-mitigation) cost and schedule impact values with the costs and timescales for the mitigation plans, so that the values for either probability or impact, or both, are updated.
- Reconcile the cost and time impacts in the fallback plan within the MR as a result of completing a more detailed analysis of fallback plans.
- Allocate an EVT to each activity or task – this information is then fed back to the risk register to ensure the RMA progress can be tracked.
- Link risks to the risk schedule.
- Run the schedule flat (with no uncertainty or risk) to check if any single-point milestone dates have altered.
- Run CRA/SRA with the risks and uncertainty included.
- Decide and agree on the schedule and cost level of MR as well as the amount of project risk exposure.
- The agreed risk appetite for cost and schedule reserve will be made up of the PMB, plus the amount of specific MR.
- Reconcile the amount of the cost and schedule buffer from the uncertainty-only calculations in the MR and review/adjust any mitigation plans as appropriate. Check that milestones and logic has not changed in the WBS.
- If required, allocate specific amounts of the MR to specific activities or tasks and create an audit trail to link these together.
- Run the risk schedule flat for a second time after reconciliation to check milestones have not altered.
- The risk appetite should be reviewed as part of both an internal and external process (for example the IBR) before setting the baseline and the MR.
- The difference between the overall confidence figure (uncertainty only) and the deterministic result is the amount of MR allocated to the project. N.B. this is kept at project level – it is consumed as the entire project progresses.

Outputs

Following these reviews, the following should be updated:

* reconciled specific risk MR;
* the schedule;
* risk register;
* reconciled values for the uncertainty buffer, mitigation actions and fallback controls.

Non-specific risk provision (or non-specific MR)

Inputs

This includes the points above as well as:

* the project's performance management reports;
* concerns register;
* as-built schedules from previous projects.

Methods

The following points illustrate how to calculate the Non Specific Risk Provision (NSRP) element of the MR. NSRP is the amount of MR that has not yet been allocated to a specific set of risks; emergent, existing or as yet unidentified.

* review the risk register(s) from previous, similar projects to highlight any systemic risks and/or issues, the project risk register maturity, project context and programme context (if appropriate);
* conduct forensic delay analysis to identify emergent risks;
* review project performance data for emergent risks;
* capture risk data, fallback plans, costs and timescales and identify as emergent risks;
* use the process for calculating the specific MR to evaluate the non-specific MR;
* reconcile the MR between specific and non-specific as any emergent risks are confirmed as live;
* update the PMB using the latest performance and risk data;
* calculate the new risk appetite for the project.

Advantages

The project manager has an amount of MR which can be drawn upon for emergent risks.

Disadvantages

Having a non-specific risk provision may inflate a contract price when some of the emergent risks do not occur. This may result in a less competitive price at the bidding stage.

8.5 Taking into account issues and outstanding risk in the prediction of likely project performance

The prediction of likely project performance is a forecast of cost and schedule outturn. It uses two major sets of data – the EV data and the data derived from projected risk impact and the draw-down/burn-up profile for the MR. The forecast of total project outturn for the cost and schedule is calculated using the following equation:

$$EAC_{MR} = EAC_{SRP} + EAC_{NSrP}$$

$$EAC_{CBB} = EAC_{PMB} + EAC_{MR}$$

It contains both the specific and non-specific elements of MR.

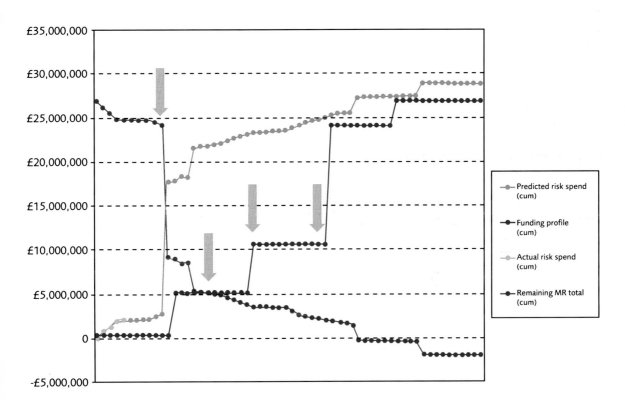

Figure 24: Forecasting – Management Reserve drawdown
Reproduced with kind permission from the APM Planning, Monitoring and Control Specific Interest Group working group

Figure 24 shows the actual MR spend against the planned baseline MR drawdown. This spend variance can be used to predict likely future spend and whether the amount of MR is sufficient to complete the project. It should be used in conjunction with a risk retirement profile that shows how many risks are planned to be retired or if their impact is to be reduced to a tolerable level.

The MR prediction must be used in conjunction with the predictions of schedule variance and EAC. A comparison can be made between predicted future events, for example, major milestones or ends of a specific phase from the EV data, with that from the MR graph. Following the latest update of EV and risk data, any of the following five things may have occurred:

1. **entire schedule slip/advance** – the schedule tasks and/or activities have moved either earlier or later than in the previous updates. The MR profile has completely shifted either earlier or later, but its profile has not changed (the project scope and risk impacts have not changed);
2. **schedule slip/advance** – as detailed above, but the MR profile changes because either tasks or activities have moved in the schedule that have risks attached to them. However, risk impact values have not changed;
3. **risk impacts and schedule tasks/activities** – both these have changed. This includes the drawdown of MR as risks impact as well as the effect of approved baseline changes;
4. **specific risks** – risks from within the register have either impacted earlier than expected or have not impacted as anticipated;
5. **non-specific risks** – these may include but not be limited to: inflation, additional foreign exchange rate rises not originally captured and additional regulatory changes arising from new legislation. If these risks impact they can be more clearly articulated and quantified. When these risks have been analysed, the budget should be moved from non-specific to specific risk provision.

In all cases, it is suggested the following checks should be made:

- check if the MR (specific and non-specific risk provision) runs out before project completion, given the current level of performance and estimates to complete;
- identify emergent risks/issues from current performance data;
- identify if any accruals are needed as a result of the latest risk and EV data;
- identify those risks that MR is being spent on;
- identify if additional MR is required and the time when this may be required. The source of these funds should also be identified;
- identify any need to change risk cost and schedule impact priorities because of project performance;
- identify if any trade-offs can be made between time, cost and quality;
- identify any opportunities that may be capitalised on to reduce the amount of MR required.

8.6 Allowing for risk in the evaluation and authorisation of project changes

As part of the change control process during the evaluation phase, the following should be done:

* use the project risk management process to identify which tasks/activities will be affected by the change;
* identify if any existing specific risks will be affected if the change is introduced;
* establish whether the change introduces new risk;
* if a new risk is introduced, use the project risk management process to incorporate it into the existing risk register;
* reconcile the risk cost and schedule impacts into the MR and prioritise as necessary;
* it is suggested that the process in Risk management section 8.3 is re-run to provide a draft update of the risk appetite and MR status. This will provide stakeholders with an understanding of the implications that the change will make to the PMB and MR;
* once the change has been approved, update the risk register, incorporate any new tasks/activities to the master schedule and complete the reconciliation process as detailed in Risk management section 8.3 on page 118 to update the risk schedule, the risk appetite and the project MR.

8.7 The effectiveness of the integration of risk and earned value management in a specific company or project

The effectiveness of the integration of EV and risk relates to the maturity of the organisation, how it reviews its performance and how it views continuous improvement. For example how is RM contributing to effective and efficient management decision making?

The maturity of RM integration with EV can be gauged by using a maturity model, for example the APM Earned Value Management Compass. This is valuable in establishing the as-is position and the aspired 'to-be' status.

Risk management process adherence
The project should be subject to regular, audit, compliance and external reporting checks. An important consideration is that personnel should be able to identify what is happening to any corrective actions that are raised as a result of these checks.

Where relevant and appropriate, the identification and escalation of systemic issues and risks should be provided to senior management for resolution.

9 Systems review

9.1 The definition of an integrated baseline review and its purpose

In order to review the quality of the developed baseline plan, an *integrated baseline review (IBR)* should be held as soon as possible after the project has gone through at least one reporting cycle following the establishment of the initial baseline. This ensures that performance data is available during the review.

An IBR is a formal process conducted to assess the content and integrity of the PMB. It should ensure the timely establishment of the integrated technical, cost and schedule baseline. It determines the credibility, sufficiency and adequacy of the planning, and ensures that activities are integrated with each other. The ultimate purpose of the IBR is to achieve and maintain a project, as well as aid customer understanding of the risks inherent in the PMB and the management control processes that will operate during its execution.

The conduct of the review process should not be restricted to project personnel but should cover all personnel, both project and customer, that are critical to the successful achievement of the project's objectives.

The purpose of an integrated baseline review is to provide the customer and contractor with an opportunity to gauge the progress made in implementing an effective EV-based project control system (PCS) and after EVM data has been generated. Fundamentally, the review should assess the progress being made towards:

* establishing a performance management baseline (PMB) that incorporates the entire scope of the project;
* scheduling the work to meet the project's objectives;
* identifying the risks/opportunities to the project along with the actions/strategies necessary to manage their impact;
* developing an understanding of the range and scale of resources required;
* implementing suitable management control processes;
* complying with an agreed EVMS guideline.

This review should involve all areas of the organisation that support a successful project controls environment, for example the finance and commercial functions.

The IBR focuses on the initial validity of the baseline plan, the resources to ensure that all scope has been planned in an achievable manner, and that management processes have been defined.

The ratio of time looking into each section of an EVMS is shown below. These figures are illustrative and act as a starting point for those reviewers new to an IBR. The percentages may be amended to suit a specific project context:

* organisation – 10%;
* schedule and resourcing – 40%;
* budget and authorisation – 10%;
* sub-contracts – 5%;
* accounts – 3%;
* analysis – 2%;
* change management – 5%;
* risk – 10%;
* effective behaviours – 10%;
* PCS team – 5%.

9.2 The definition of a demonstration review and its purpose

In order to examine the new project management system, a demonstration review may be held. This is different from an IBR because it reviews the total system, looking particularly at the system operations. The EVMS is checked fully for compliance against all the earned value criteria.

In addition to the EVMS review, data traces and interviews are undertaken. Covering areas that play a role in operating the system are included, such as finance and project controls, as well as the managers.

This time, the EVMS is assessed against all the EV guidelines. The demonstration review report is written during the review, based on the five guideline groups of:

- organisation;
- planning, scheduling and budgeting;
- accounting;
- analysis and management reports;
- revisions and data maintenance.

It highlights where the system is working well and addresses the discrepancy reports on system deficiencies.

The demonstration review is undertaken once the programme has been using EVM data for at least six months post-integrated baseline review (IBR).

The scope of the review is the same as an IBR, but with a particular focus on the use of the project controls data supporting the decision making process. The ratio of time looking into each section of an EVMS would be:

- organisation – 5%;
- schedule and resourcing – 10%;   *System Review*
- budget and authorisation – 5%;
- sub-contracts – 15%;
- accounts – 10%;
- analysis – 25%;
- change management – 15%;
- risk – 5%;
- effective behaviours – 5%;
- project control system team – 5%.

128

9.3 The definition of surveillance and its purpose

In order to confirm that standards are being maintained, periodic surveillance should be conducted throughout the remainder of the project.

Like any dynamic control system, there is always a possibility that the project may run out of control: with an EVMS, it can sometimes be easy for the project to fall into complacency and let the management system run without doing any further data checks highlighting any data integrity problems. At this stage of the project there are likely to have been substantial changes made to the project's system. These will include changes aimed at improving the system which will need to be reviewed to ensure they are still in accordance with the EV guidelines of the criteria set out in Appendix A. in the *Earned Value Management: APM Guidelines* (APM, 2008)

There is also the possibility that both management and CAMs have undergone considerable change. New managers need to be interviewed to ensure that they are fully conversant with the management of earned value.

Surveillance must ensure that the project's EVMS:

- provides timely and reliable cost, schedule and technical performance information summarised directly from the project's internal management system;
- complies with the EVM guidelines;
- provides timely indications of actual or potential problems;
- maintains baseline integrity;
- provides information that depicts actual conditions and trends;
- provides comprehensive variance analysis at the appropriate levels, including proposed corrective action with regard to cost, schedule and technical performance, and other problem areas.

A surveillance review is normally undertaken when there has been a significant change to the baseline or when more than 12 months have passed since the demonstration review.

The focus of the surveillance review is to ensure that the project controls environment is robust and that the data provided is of a sufficient quality to enable effective decisions.

9.4 The process for an integrated baseline review

The tables on pages 130-131 describe the overall process for establishing and conducting an integrated baseline review (IBR). It follows an overall route map as outlined below.

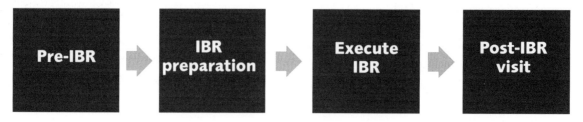

Figure 25: The IBR Process diagram
Reproduced with kind permission from the APM Planning, Monitoring and Control Specific Interest Group working group

The major inputs, outputs, processes and responsibilities are outlined in the following table:

The process description and discussion for all four elements of the process follow after the table.

Input	Process	Output	Responsibility
New contract/contract change/ company policy/ significant project change.	Decision to hold an IBR.	Documented decision – contract, project plan, etc.	Contractual responsibility or joint or internal responsibility?
IBR guideline. Contract.	Agree objectives and the acceptance/success criteria.	Notification of the IBR and timing, the plan (including objectives, acceptance criteria and expectations) for the IBR and success criteria and/or measures of success.	Customer lead and project manager.

Table 18: Pre-IBR

Scope month 2

Input	Process	Output	Responsibility
Skills and competencies. IBR plan and available resources.	Identify teams and team composition.	Contact list generated, roles and responsibilities agreed.	Customer lead and project manager.
This study guide. IBR plan and project control. System description.	Produce the draft IBR briefing pack/handbook.	The draft IBR briefing pack/ handbook.	Customer lead and project manager.
Team knowledge, skills and abilities. Training resources.	Educate teams (reviewers and project team).	Competent team members.	Customer lead and project manager.
Project data.	Mock/practice IBR.	Issues for resolution prior to the IBR.	Project manager.
Availability, resources and locations.	Define and agree visit schedule.	Timetable.	Customer lead and project manager.
Review team requirements.	Administration and domestics.	Included in the IBR handbook as appropriate.	Project manager.
	Produce final IBR handbook.	Final IBR handbook.	Customer lead and project manager.
Baseline data and documentation. IBR handbook.	Collate and deliver IBR deliverables.	Documentation issued to review team.	Project manager.
Documentation with review team.	Review and familiarise with deliverables.	Review team ready.	Review team.

Table 19: IBR preparation   Demonstration → check EVMS

130

Input	Process	Output	Responsibility
Agenda.	In-brief and launch.	Fully briefed team.	Joint responsibility.
IBR documentation, data requests and the storyboard.	Data traces, assessment of project control system description e.g. against IBR 32 guideline criteria or the Earned Value Compass.	Write-ups.	Review team.
CAM specific data.	CAM/manager discussions.	Write-ups.	Review team.
Write-ups.	Collate write-ups (to be progressed throughout execution).	Topic write-ups.	Review team.
Write-ups.	Feedback sessions/issues board.	Daily issues raised with the project team.	Review team.
Issues and write-ups.	Review closure.	Out-brief presentation material and corrective action plan.	Joint responsibility.

Table 20: Execute IBR

Input	Process	Output	Responsibility
IBR report.	Prepare and agree actions for closure of corrective actions.	Corrective action closure plan.	Project manager and review team.
Feedback form.	Post-review feedback.	Completed feedback form, and lessons learnt documentation.	Project manager and review team.
Corrective action closure plan.	Joint surveillance.	Agreed schedule and type of future reviews.	Review sponsor and project manager.
IBR report.	Prepare and agree actions for closure of corrective actions.	Corrective action closure plan.	Project manager and review team.
Feedback form.	Post-review feedback.	Completed feedback form, and lessons learnt documentation.	Project manager and review team.
Corrective action closure plan.	Joint surveillance.	Agreed schedule and type of future reviews.	Review sponsor and project manager.

Table 21: Post-IBR visit

9.4.1 Making the decision to hold an IBR

The factors that drive the requirement to conduct the IBR process are outlined in the document *A Guide to Conducting Integrated Baseline Reviews* (2009). They are also included in Table 18 on page 131. As noted, an initial review should be conducted as soon as practicable after the project authorisation.

Ideally, the schedule of reviews will have been planned and agreed in advance. However, significant events that affect the project may also trigger the requirement for a review, for example:

- new contract;
- contract change;
- company policy;
- significant project change;
- process;
- organisation;
- work content scope;
- time-phasing;
- funding (annual and total).

9.4.2 Agree objectives and acceptance criteria

As soon as the decision to conduct an IBR has been made the project manager and the customer should agree and define the specific objectives and acceptance criteria for the review. This agreement may be documented in an initial draft of the project IBR handbook.

To assess the PMB it needs to be established that the following have been achieved:

- assumptions underlying the plan are reasonable and documented;
- project requirements have been translated into appropriate breakdown structures and authorised through documents such as work breakdown structure (WBS) and statement of work (SoW);
- project schedule key milestones are identified and reflect a logical flow to accomplish technical work scope;
- the project organisation is identified and a clear responsibility link to the WBS is shown e.g. responsibility assignment matrix (RAM);
- the planned use of resources (budgets, facilities, personnel, skills, etc.) reflects the required availability and is sufficient to accomplish the technical scope of work within schedule constraints over the entire performance period;
- the sub-contract effort and performance reporting is integrated to the level that is effective for project control;
- the earned value measurement techniques (EVMTs) applied are appropriate to the scope of work being undertaken in order for the project performance data to reflect project achievement during the entire performance period.

The risk areas detailed below should be assessed.

Technical risk: the ability of the contractor to fulfil the customer requirements (e.g. contract, SoW) and the product to meet performance requirements, technology and technology-readiness levels;

Schedule risk: the critical path, vertical and horizontal integration, logical sequence of events and the correct use of scheduling constraints should all be assessed. Schedule risk analysis (SRA) should also be checked to give confidence that the contractor can deliver to the agreed schedule.

Management control processes: to establish the degree to which effective technical/schedule/cost planning and management control processes exist and have been implemented.

Cost risk: the assessment should determine whether there is sufficient MR to address the risk items and assumptions identified. Confirm whether resources are sufficient to meet performance requirements, and that they support the schedule, as well as whether the resources will be available in the timescales necessary to support the schedule. The status of funding authorisation (internal and/or external) should also be reviewed.

Supplier management: assess and confirm that key suppliers and sub-contractors are able to deliver their commitments to time, quality and cost. The assessment should determine how system/reporting requirements have been placed on the suppliers, and how the integration of sub-contract baseline/achievement/costs will be achieved.

Having taken project specifics into account and agreed the IBR objectives, care should be exercised in order to ensure that all parties involved are aware of the approach to be taken in conducting the review.

To formalise the review, the customer should prepare an IBR notification letter which includes review dates, team members, review conduct, documentation required and any other pertinent information. This letter should be sent to team members and the contractor.

9.4.3 Preparation

9.4.3.1 Identify teams

Reviews should be led by a suitably qualified and experienced person, who will provide a suitably qualified team to ensure that a comprehensive evaluation of the PMB is performed and that all project control aspects have been addressed and captured.

Team members for the review should include a mixture of the project's engineering and technical staff, with support from the project control specialists. Project staff should be knowledgeable on the subject matter being examined. All team members will be allocated specific WBS areas of responsibility, ideally associated with their field of expertise and project management responsibility. It is important that a multi-functional IBR team's project knowledge is transferred among all participants.

9.4.3.2 Responsibilities

Table 22 outlines the responsibilities of the various stakeholders involved in the IBR.

Project manager/customer (jointly responsible for IBR process).	• Agree the objectives and schedule for the IBR process and supporting reviews. • Ensure an adequate number of suitably qualified and experienced personnel are available to support the IBR process. • Ensure issues resulting from reviews are resolved in a timely manner.
Team leaders/project managers as appropriate.	• Provide technical direction and leadership. • Assign responsibilities to review team members. • Ensure team members are adequately trained and prepared for reviews. • Day to day management of the IBR process and reviews.
Team members.	• Be prepared for the review and attend IBR training workshops. • Familiarise themselves with the SoW or statement of requirements/objectives prior to the review. • Review the project's planning documentation and undertake data traces. • Conduct discussions. • Provide write-up assessments and contribute to the final review report.
Project.	• Provide the appropriate planning documentation to the team for review prior to the start of the IBR. • Provide working space and support for the IBR team. • Arrange schedules for discussions with relevant project personnel.

Table 22: IBR responsibilities for review team members
Reproduced with kind permission from the APM Planning, Monitoring and Control Specific Interest Group working group

Review teams may allocate responsibilities to team leads for documenting various elements of the final report, organised by process element. The team lead will therefore have to collate all the relevant elements of the CAM discussions, data traces, etc. for amalgamation into the report.

9.4.3.3 Team composition

The project manager/customer should identify the team leader(s) and members. Individuals selected for the IBR team should be experienced in both project management and the technical disciplines under review.

The team should include experienced personnel who are independent of the project. The following are areas of discipline that should be represented in the team. Please note that this is not an exhaustive list:

• project management;
• project control;
• business management;
• sub-contract management;
• technical management;
• contract management.

The size of the team and duration of the review should be appropriate to the project size and its complexity.

9.4.3.4 Draft IBR briefing pack/handbook

A briefing pack or handbook should be produced which covers all aspects from this guide that are applicable to the review in question. This will ensure that everyone involved has a clear understanding of the expectations, conduct and timing of the review.

9.4.3.5 Educate teams (reviewers and project team)

Joint training sessions should be held wherever practicable for all personnel involved in the review, either as reviewers or members of the project team to review. The training's goal is to provide enough information so the team can understand the cost, schedule, technical, and management processes used on the project. When necessary, it may be appropriate to bring in external personnel for training and facilitation.

Training should be designed and delivered to support the objectives of the review as agreed by the project managers. The essential elements of the training should include the following areas:

Review team training

- **project control training**
It is important that review teams are adequately versed in project control disciplines. As an absolute minimum, training courses on the basics of project control and the analysis of data should be provided for all personnel associated with the review;

- **review methodology training**
Review team members should be adequately trained for their role. This training should include discussion techniques, data tracing processes and how to document findings and issues;

- **project familiarisation**
The review team should familiarise themselves with project specifics and dynamics including:

  - review the handbook/briefing pack;
  - review leader's expectations;
  - project organisation;
  - budget baseline;
  - schedule baseline;
  - funding issues (sources, constraints and timing);
  - scope of work/statement of requirements/objectives;
  - risk identification and documentation;
  - sub-contractor(s) management;
  - procurement;
  - change management;
  - reporting.

- **joint project/review team training**
Many projects will conduct training sessions within the normal system operation and processes. Where the project provides such training, the review team may seek to participate in these training opportunities.

- **project team training**
The project manager/team will need to prepare for the review by training appropriate project personnel in the process and conduct of a review.

A series of communication briefings may be conducted to ensure all personnel involved in the review are aware of the overall review objectives, processes, timings and any activities that need to be completed in readiness for the review. It is important that the review is given the necessary priority by all stakeholders, particularly control account managers (CAMs) and the project management team.

9.4.3.6 Mock/practice IBR

To assist in the preparation of a review, a mock or practice review may be held. This may completely replicate the entire scope of the IBR, or could focus on preparing the IBR team with particular attention/emphasis toward the CAM.

In order to prepare the CAM(s), and to ensure that they are fully effective during the IBR discussion, projects often provide IBR coaching. This could take the form of mock discussions, conducted by independent personnel, which would follow the format agreed for the real review with feedback provided to the CAM regarding their performance and any areas for improvement. The mock discussion may also identify areas in the CAM's data that need to be developed further, prior to the review.

Data tracing should be undertaken as part of a mock review to identify any potential problem areas that subsequently can be briefed to the review team.

9.4.3.7 Define and agree visit schedule

The major activities of the IBR will include:

* in-brief for the review team explaining the purpose of the review and providing the opportunity for the introduction of all team members;
* an overview by the project – to familiarise the team with the characteristics of the EVM;
* the review of project planning data, including system data traces and review of the project control system description (PCSD) or equivalent and any associated project directives or instructions that support the PCSD;
* discussions with CAM(s) identifying the basis on which the plan was established, ensuring that resources have been allocated and that appropriate performance measurement techniques have been identified;
* an exception report addressing the review team's concerns and findings. All concerns requiring resolution should be identified and, if not already resolved prior to completion of the IBR, the estimated dates for resolution should be agreed;
* a joint exit briefing by the review team addressing the team's review findings.

Working hours may vary slightly during the review, depending on the particular activities being undertaken. It is assumed that each day will commence with a team meeting held in an IBR office and will conclude at the close of business, which is defined as the completion of the following activities:

* completion of all activities scheduled for the day;
* reports of discussions conducted;
* project office daily de-briefs.

Figure 26 shows a generic agenda for an IBR.

Generic agenda

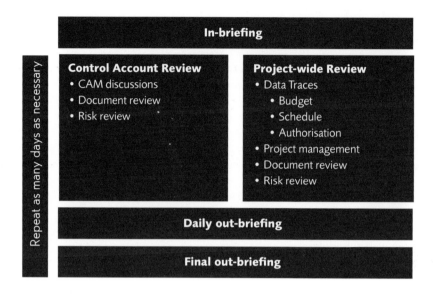

Figure 26: A generic IBR agenda
Reproduced with kind permission from BAE SYSTEMS Ltd

Day 1:

0900 – 1000	Review team In-brief
1020 – 1230	Project presentation (overview) and documentation review
1230 – 1330	Lunch
1330 – 1700	Documentation review, data traces and schedule review
1700 – Close	Project de-brief of the day's findings

Days 2, 3 and 4 (if required):

0830 – 1000	Documentation review/data traces, CAM preparation
1000 – 1200	CAM discussion session
1200 – 1230	Team discussion
1230 – 1330	Lunch
1330 – 1430	Documentation review/data traces, CAM preparation
1430 – 1630	CAM discussion session
1630 – 1700	Team discussion
1700 - Close	Project de-brief of the day's findings

Days 4 and 5 (if required):

0830 – 1230	Documentation review/data traces, follow-up actions from previous days, consolidation of the review team's findings
1230 – 1330	Lunch
1330 – 1430	IBR results to project director

- **Administration**

The IBR will require a certain amount of administration to ensure its smooth path for the benefit of all stakeholders. The administrative requirements will usually include:

- ensuring visitors (the review team) are cleared for any security requirements, and that arrangements are in place for them to be collected/escorted while on site;
- providing working space and support for the IBR team including a working area and administrative support as required;
- arranging schedules for discussions with CAM(s) and other project management staff and ensure all personnel are available;
- ensuring that rooms for CAM discussions are available – ideally the CAM's own work environment.

9.4.3.8 Produce final IBR handbook

The draft IBR handbook should be finalised and issued to all stakeholders, to ensure that they have an unambiguous understanding of the intent, objectives, process and timetable for the review.

9.4.3.9 Collate and complete IBR deliverables

The following documentation should be provided to the review team prior to the review and far enough in advance for the team to familiarise themselves with their content:

- statement of work (SoW);
- Project Management Plan (PMP);
- WBS and dictionary;
- project organisational structure;
- responsibility assignment matrix (RAM);
- work authorisation documents;
- programme schedules, including contract master schedule and detail schedules that support control accounts (CA);
- schedule risk analysis (SRA);
- risk and opportunities log;
- control account (CA) plans or equivalent;
- records documenting contractual changes and internal actions;
- current EV performance report (if available at the time of the first review);
- project control management system;
- a list of major sub-contractors and major vendors, including description of product, applicable WBS element, value of sub-contracts/purchase orders, period of performance, and responsible CAM;
- basic contract and any modifications.

In order to reduce the amount of paperwork, it may be possible to transfer this material over a shared data environment. Alternative methods such as electronic (CD/DVD) deliverables may also be appropriate, depending on commercial and security constraints.

9.4.4 Execution

When reviewing the PMB and associated system documentation a distinction should be made between the acceptability of the intended approach (as defined in any policy or process documentation) and the extent to which that approach is being effectively employed.

The final report will usually consist of a number of process-related sections, for example organisation, scheduling, budgeting etc., plus any corrective action reports that may have been raised. Responsibility for compiling these sections should be allocated to team members. This approach assists in timely report preparation.

9.4.4.1 In-brief and launch

The in-brief is an opportunity for the review team to gain an understanding of the project being reviewed. This may include:

* a group introduction/communication session (for familiarisation purposes);
* a site tour;
* overview of the project;
* making the review team aware of known project control system deficiencies and actions in hand.

9.4.4.2 Data traces

Data tracing is an important component of any review and is a methodology for tracing a source data element through the EVMS, as well as understanding how the overall system operates. When conducting traces, evidence must be documented. In some cases, the team leader may request that examples of the trace be obtained.

The following data traces should be considered during the review:

* project control system description comparison with the relevant project control guidance document, for example, the *Earned Value Management: APM Guidelines* (APM, 2008), ANSI 748 or the *Earned Value Management Compass* (APM, 2010);
* organisation/authorisation trace;
* schedule trace including sub-contractors;
* budget trace;
* labour trace;
* material trace;
* status trace, for example progress/performance status;
* risk and opportunity traces;
* change management controls trace.

One of the objectives of the review is to ensure traceability throughout the system. If any inconsistencies or anomalies are apparent, they should be addressed on the CA and CAM evaluation sheets. Guidance on the conduct of data traces may be found in *A Guide to Conducting Integrated Baseline Reviews* (2009).

9.4.4.3 Control Account Manager/manager discussions

A key feature of the IBR is the conduct of discussions by the review team on a sample group of CAMs and functional managers, for example, finance, human resources and commercial. Senior management and other stakeholders should also be engaged in this process.

Depending on the organisational structure of the contractor, there may be value in conducting interviews with other personnel in the contractor's office, such as functional managers, team leaders and the project manager. The functional manager and team leader interviews will focus on their role in relation to the CAM regarding assistance with the schedule, resourcing, review of risks and the review of progress. These managers may be responsible for several CAMs.

The project manager interview will focus on risks, MR, reporting mechanisms within the contractor's office and the project manager's confidence in the PMB and the EVMS. The project manager should provide details on the risk management structures and responsibilities and these should be verified through interviews with other managers.

An interview with the finance manager should be conducted to verify the manner in which overheads/indirect costs have been applied to the contract.

The objective of these discussions is to enable the review team to understand the methods and reasoning for how the PMB has been developed, is/will be maintained and how performance data will be used to manage the project. The particular questions that should be asked should take account of the following:

- the structure of the particular project's control system;
- any risks/issues known to the review team prior to the review;
- any risks/issues identified from documentation reviews prior to the discussion.

Prior to each discussion, the review team should familiarise themselves with the following information/documents relating to the CAM in question:

- budgetary information from the RAM;
- CA definition and authorisation documents;
- WP definitions and associated budget structures;
- schedules;
- performance reports if available.

It is sometimes possible to use a dedicated part of the review team to undertake pre-discussion data scrubs. This involves an offline review of the CAM folder, highlighting any areas of inconsistency or concern. This is documented and briefed to the review team member who has responsibility for the interview. A sample data scrub checklist is provided in *A Guide to Conducting Integrated Baseline Reviews* (2009).

The following is a guide to the preparation required before an IBR CAM discussion:

- check the schedule for the name of your first CAM interviewee;
- find their location on the organisation chart and RAM;
- determine their responsibility area on the WBS;
- what does that SoW entail? Check the WBS, dictionary, and other documentation where the work is described;

- is the total work effort consistent with the SoW?
- how many CAs do they have? What are the values? Check the costed RAM for this data;
- identify the work authorisation document that authorises the CAM to do the work. It should show the work they are authorised to do, a schedule to do the work in, a CA or WP number to charge the work to, and a budget for performing the work;
- review the CAM's authorising documentation. The work, schedule, CA number and budget should be consistent with that authorised on the work authorisation document;
- review the sufficiency of the allocated CA budgets, both in terms of work content, total resources and time-phasing;
- contractors will transform data from the CA plan to an internal computer data system. Review the outputs of this data to ensure it correlates to the CAM's plan;
- review the methods the CAM is using to take BCWP (earned value techniques). This may be shown on the CA plan or similar. Any BCWP being reported to the authority on the cost performance report (CPR), should be consistent and reconcilable to the internal BCWP;
- trace the CA schedule to the next higher level schedule and check that the dates and milestones agree;
- check to see if the CAM made any changes to their CA plan. If so, find the change that authorised this.

The number of CAM discussions that need to be conducted and the choice of CAMs and/or managers should be decided in order to achieve an acceptable level of confidence that the sample is indicative of the overall project performance. Particular attention should be given to any areas of the PMB or functional departments that the review team believes pose the greatest risk to the successful achievement of the project's objectives.

Discussions should be conducted in a non-confrontational manner and should be treated as a joint exercise for the benefit of both parties.

The discussion team should normally consist of no more than two representatives from the review team, one leading and asking the questions, the other taking notes and ensuring all areas have been covered. It is recommended that a representative from the project who has overall knowledge of the system is present as an observer to pick up any generic system issues. Where either the review team or project team wish to add further observers, care should be taken not to detract from the objectives of the discussion or put either party in a position of unease. There may be occasions where the reviewers will need to include a technical peer to the CAM in the interview to test the basis of estimate, scheduling, budget and risk.

A *Guide to Conducting Integrated Baseline Reviews* (2009) provides example questions that could be asked during the discussions.

9.4.4.4 CAM discussion guidance

Where possible the review should take place in the CAM's work area. This ensures a friendly environment and provides the opportunity for evidence not immediately to hand to be quickly located by the CAM. Phrase questions so that they can be easily understood and that they cannot be answered by a simple yes or no and utilise the 'show me' technique. Structure the discussion in such a manner to allow the interviewee enough room to discuss freely how they follow the process. The CAM should use documents when answering questions. If the CAM struggles to understand a question, try to rephrase without using jargon. Remember that some CAMs will be in training and this does not necessarily mean that they do not understand the technical scope and plan for their work.

If required, ask for relevant documents that are referenced. Keep in mind the need to document the work, and what is expected as adequate evidence of your conclusions on the overall scope. If documentation is requested, but cannot be made available until after the discussion, be sure to get a commitment regarding when the data will be made available. This information is only to substantiate the CAM's claim.

Most importantly, treat the CAM as you would like to be treated if it was you in the same situation.

9.4.4.5 After the CAM discussion

Immediately following the discussion, the interview notes should be compiled into observations and the CA/CAM evaluation sheets should be completed – an example may be found in *A Guide to Conducting Integrated Baseline Reviews* (2009) should be completed. It is recommended that reviewers maintain their own discussion files to keep notes for subsequent write-ups, which can be then referred to, along with other data you may compile to complete the total write-up for the assigned CWBS area. Follow up on data requests if they are slow in being honoured.

The team leaders will review the corrective action report (CARs) sheets, an example may be found in *A Guide to Conducting Integrated Baseline Reviews* (2009), and if considered necessary, will present them to the contractor to be resolved. It is the responsibility of the various review team members to ensure that they prepare well-documented CARs.

9.4.4.6 Collate write-ups

Results of the CAM discussions should be recorded on the evaluation sheets. An example may be found in *A Guide to Conducting Integrated Baseline Reviews* (2009). It should have been agreed at the outset whether or not these reports will be part of the review report.

9.4.4.7 Feedback sessions/issues board

It is beneficial to maintain a live issues board during the review and to feed back key findings on a daily basis. This will provide all review team members with an overview of how the review is progressing and enable the findings to be addressed before the end of the review.

9.4.4.8 Review closure

After completion of a review, a wash-up meeting should be held with all project stakeholders in order to agree any relevant key findings and subsequent actions. The project manager/customer should agree on a plan of closeout actions and who is responsible for the action. These actions should be considered as project risks/issues and treated accordingly.

Reporting the results of the review may take the form of an informal letter or memo. The letter should address any action items that have been agreed between the contractor and customer/client. Where applicable it should summarise the findings that require corrective action and assign the surveillance of the corrective action to the project manager.

9.4.5 Post-visit

9.4.5.1 Corrective action plan

At the conclusion of the onsite IBR activity, all concerns requiring resolution should be identified with an estimated date for resolution proposed by the project review team.

Depending on the number and severity of the findings, the project team may need to identify a date by which a corrective action plan will be provided to address the findings. Where only a few findings exist, the team may be in a position to provide dates against each item immediately. The corrective action plan should provide sufficient detail to allow the IBR team leader to review the adequacy of the proposed solution. These corrective actions will need to be tracked to closure prior to final approval of the PMB.

Any additional risks/issues identified during the IBR should be recorded in the internal risk/issues log and managed accordingly. The IBR team leader should also ensure that the project team has taken appropriate action to record any risks/issues identified during the IBR process.

9.4.5.2 Post-review feedback

In order to support the continuous improvement of the IBR process, a post-IBR conduct review should be carried out; annex H of *A Guide to Conducting Integrated Baseline Reviews* (2009) may be used for this purpose. This will provide feedback to the review team regarding the success of the review process from the participants' point of view. Findings should be passed on to other review teams in order to improve the process wherever possible.

9.4.5.3 Joint surveillance

The IBR may be the only review required. The need for any other type of review to re-assess the EVMS may be evaluated by the customer representative in conjunction with the project manager. The plan for EVM surveillance activities should be based upon the degree of risk identified during the IBR and the degree to which the EVMS satisfies contractual requirements.

9.5 The process for a demonstration review

Considerations
The decision to hold a demonstration review
A demonstration review (DR) is usually held after at least four reporting periods have been completed. This allows the management team to capture the minimum amount of information to start looking for trends in the performance data and to identify:

* any systemic issues with data generation;
* any systemic issues with the EV processes being deployed;
* any issues with the way in which decisions are being made;
* any issues that affect the closure of any IBR CARs;
* any issues that prevent an improvement in EV and project control maturity within the project and/or organisation.

The process for a DR is very similar to that detailed in section 9.4 on page 129.
It may use appropriate elements of the IBR review process. The table in section 9. may be used for this purpose.

Areas that may not have been covered in detail during an IBR will include change control/management and analysis, review and action. Particular attention needs to be paid to these as the EVMS begins to be used on a regular basis.

This review covers the entire EVMS and is assessed against all the EVMS guidelines.
The focus of the demonstration review is to ensure that there is good data integrity, that the data is being used to inform project decision making and that the PMB is still robust. The review is typically carried out several months after the IBR.

Observation of the monthly project performance reviews can also be used to assess whether the data is being used for project decision making.

9.6 The process for a surveillance review

Considerations

The process used for a surveillance review follows the same steps as those of the IBR and DR.
A systems review should be implemented when the project's EVMS is showing a number of data integrity issues.

Any changes and improvements that may have been made to the EVMS need to be taken into account. These changes will need to be checked to ensure the EVMS still meets the guidelines used in the IBR and in the contract.

9.7 The process of a readiness review

Considerations

These reviews determine whether the organisation to be reviewed in depth is in fact ready to be reviewed. It identifies what needs to happen in order for the organisation to be ready to receive a formal inspection. This avoids the situation where review team resources are committed to attending and then find that the organisation is not yet ready to be reviewed.

A readiness review, usually led by a person independent from the project, will help the project team understand what it needs to do to plan for a successful IBR. Success will be defined in the IBR exit criteria.

Prior to the contract award, the assumption is that work undertaken by the contractor in preparing a proposal will have recognised the need (contractually or otherwise) for an effective project control system. This will then manifest itself in the documents and plans produced to date. The review should establish the progress to date and determine the key actions and timescales necessary to establish an effective system. This information will then support any decisions regarding the timing of the initial IBR.

9.8 The benefits of systems reviews

Earned value reviews provide several benefits:

1. They confirm that an integrated project management system exists.
2. They will provide a *fixed cut-off point* to conclude the planning phase.
3. They are pre-planned checkpoints. They validate reliable performance data, thus avoiding wasted subsequent work based on unsound information.
4. They reduce *risk*.
5. They should ensure that *historic experience* from previous projects is captured.
6. They can be an effective tool to put the focus on performance measurement.

9.9 Identifying the issues in the effective management of an integrated baseline review

The challenges in an IBR are as follows:

- effectively co-ordinating the outputs of the data trace to ensure that issues are followed up during interviews;
- managing the IBR team to ensure that feedback from interviews/data traces is captured and followed up adequately;
- ensuring that the IBR team is adequately trained to perform the review;
- ensuring that the review is objectively performed;
- ensuring that corrective actions are captured correctly by the IBR team and acted upon within an agreed timescale;
- ensuring that the IBR handbook is completed before the IBR;
- ensuring that any sensitive issues regarding CARs are dealt with;
- ensuring that the IBR timetable is agreed.

9.10 Identifying the issues in the effective management of a demonstration review

The issues and challenges identified in the management of an IBR are equally applicable to the DR. However, there is also the need to include greater focus on areas of:

- analysis;
- change control;
- data maintenance;
- data trace;
- interviews;
- EVMS operation and any changes to it;
- looking at the entire EVMS, not just checking that the PMB is robust.

It is also important to review the corrective actions list.

9.11 Identifying the issues in the effective management of a surveillance review

The issues and challenges identified in the management of an IBR are equally applicable to the SR. There is, however, one addition, which is that the organisation's compliance with its own EVMS policies and procedures for the project should be checked.

9.12 The effectiveness of implementing an integrated baseline review process

In order to review the quality of the developed baseline plan, an IBR should be held as soon as possible after the project has completed at least one reporting cycle, but ideally three reporting cycles, following the establishment of the initial baseline. This ensures that performance data is available during the review. It should also ensure the timely establishment of the integrated technical, cost and schedule baseline and determine the credibility, sufficiency and adequacy of the planning, as well as ensuring that activities are integrated with each other.

The ultimate purpose of the IBR is to achieve and maintain a project, as well as customer understanding of the risks inherent in the PMB and the management control processes that will operate during its execution. The conduct of the review process should not be restricted to project personnel but should cover all personnel, both project and customer, who are critical to the successful achievement of the project's objectives.

9.13 The effectiveness of implementing a demonstration review

In order to examine the new project management system, a demonstration review (DR) may be held. This is different from an IBR because it reviews the total system, looking particularly at the system operations. The EVMS is checked fully for compliance against all the EV criteria. In addition to the EVMS review, data traces and interviews are undertaken. Areas that play a role in operating the system are included, such as finance and project controls, and managers. This time, the EVMS is assessed against all the EV guidelines. The demonstration review report is written during the review, based on the five guideline groups of:

* organisation;
* planning, scheduling and budgeting;
* accounting;
* analysis and management reports;
* revisions and data maintenance.

It highlights where the system is working well and addresses the discrepancy reports on system deficiencies.

9.14 The effectiveness of implementing a surveillance review

In order to confirm that standards are being maintained, periodic surveillance should be conducted throughout the remainder of the project. Like any dynamic control system, there is always a possibility that the project may run out of control. With an EVMS, it can sometimes be easy for the project to fall into complacency and let the management system run without doing any further data checks that could highlight data integrity problems. At this stage of the project there are likely to have been substantial changes made to the project's system. These will include changes aimed at improving the system and it is important that the changes and their rationale should be documented. There is also the possibility that both management and CAMs have undergone considerable change. New managers need to be interviewed to ensure that they are fully conversant with the management of EV. System review surveillance must ensure that the project's EVMS:

* provides timely and reliable cost, schedule and technical performance information summarised directly from the project's internal management system;
* complies with the EVM guidelines;
* provides timely indications of actual or potential problems;
* maintains baseline integrity;
* provides information that depicts actual conditions and trends;
* provides comprehensive variance analysis at the appropriate levels, including proposed corrective action with regard to the cost, schedule and technical performance, as well as other problem areas.

9.15 The effectiveness of the systems review

Aspects to consider are:

- whether the benefits in section 6 of the *APM Earned Value Management Guidelines* have been achieved;
- whether the review has been set up correctly;
- whether any corrective actions have been fully identified;
- whether the corrective actions identified have been implemented.

Factors that determine when a risk cannot be managed by the project and may need escalating might include:

- when either the project or business unit does not have sufficient funds or resources to implement the mitigation action or the fallback plan should the risk materialise;
- when agreement cannot be reached across the relevant interface or within the relevant forum regarding how the risk should be managed;
- when the risk is common (or systemic) to more than one project or more than one business unit;
- when the potential impact of the risk is so great that it may significantly affect the level of business capability that can be delivered.

The mitigation action is disproportionate to the risk at project level, but may be proportionate for an equivalent risk at programme level.

10 Learning from experience

10.1 The importance of closing down a project effectively

A project does not end when the goal has been achieved and it is ready to hand over to the customer. Often there is an eagerness to move on to the next project but it is important that the project is closed effectively and to ensure that:

- all the scope has been completed;
- all documentation has been completed;
- a project review takes place before the project team is disbanded.

The project close out review is the last opportunity to capture, analyse and record the learning from experience (LFE) which can then be passed on to the next project, communicated to other projects and be readily available for future projects. The benefits of learning from experience are covered in detail in this section.

10.2 The value and impact of learning from experience

Learning from previous experience is identified by PRINCE2® as one of the seven principles:

"Lessons learned are sought, recorded and acted upon throughout the project life cycle."

Lessons are applied from previous projects or project phases in order to learn and improve the way future projects and phases are delivered. Lessons should be captured from each significant project phase or event. This learning can then be shared within the project team to improve subsequent phases, or outside the project team to improve other projects.

The benefits of an effective LFE process are:

- it helps to avoid expensive mistakes;
- it enables better project performance and execution effectiveness;
- it enables better project execution predictability;
- it provides a stronger integrated project team and project execution communities;
- it provides information for benchmarking activity/task times, costs, risks and work rate(s).

10.3 The sources of learning from experience

The two significant sources of LFE are:

1. people and their experiences on a project. For a list see section 10.8 on page 156.
2. project documents and histories. For a list see section 10.6 on page 154.

10.4 The definition of learning from experience

There are many processes, models and frameworks available to structure the process of capturing, disseminating and acting upon lessons learnt. Most are cyclical, suggesting that LFE is a recurrent process. Many focus on the individual's ability to reflect on their own learning and experience but these processes can be applied to the learning and experience of a group or team.

Figure 27: Learning from experience cycle diagram
Taken from Gibbs, G (1988) *Learning by doing. A guide to teaching and learning methods.* Oxford: Further Education.
Reproduced with kind permission from BMTHiQSigma

The nature of LFE will vary depending on where a project is in the project lifecycle. Typically a project will seek LFE during its initial stages but will give LFE in the later stages.

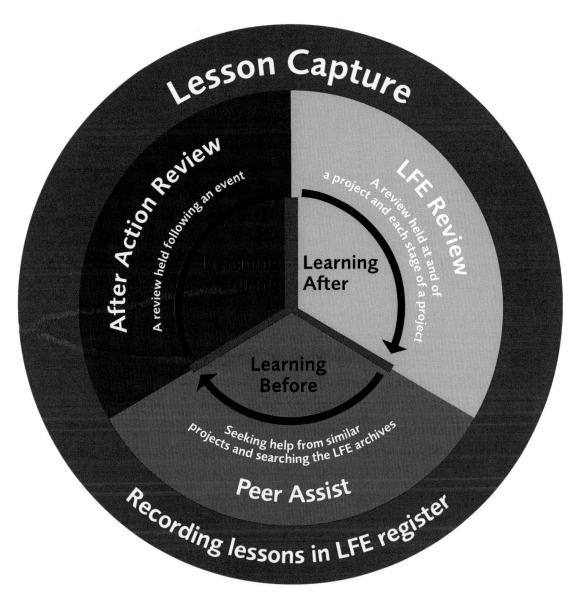

Figure 28: the nature of learning from experience
Reproduced with kind permission from Sellafield Limited

10.5 Conducting a learning from experience review

An LFE session or review is a simple tool which assists project team members learn after the completion of a project stage or at the end of the overall project. It brings together relevant team members and allows them to evaluate the outcomes of their actions and to draw lessons for the future. It is usually conducted with the help of a facilitator and is a tool for prioritising and synthesising lessons learned across the whole project lifespan.

Inputs
- The facilitator.
- Project performance data – for a phase or stage.
- Team members.
- Phase, stage, task or activity context.
- Relevant risks, issues and opportunities.
- Project history and/or diary.
- Change control history.
- Contract, plus all amendments and/or renovations and other changes where applicable.
- Previous relevant LFE elements.
- Information/knowledge repository.

Considerations
- Lessons should be agreed by all project team members.
- Try to conduct within a month of stage/project completion.
- Try to complete individual LFE elements as soon after the task/activity/stage has completed.
- Always focus on future improvements and re-usability.
- Involve all participants in the discussion.
- Use open-ended questions and encourage open and honest discussions.
- Remember all participants are equal; there is no hierarchy.
- LFE sessions should be facilitated by an independent person.
- The size and complexity of the project.
- The information and knowledge system to capture the LFE.

Methods
Brainstorm: Individuals are asked to capture their thoughts on sticky notes. Individuals can write about whatever they like, as filtering is done later. The facilitator will provide both good and bad examples of what should be written.

Figure 29 Good and bad examples of how learning from experience elements should be written

Identify themes: Flipcharts are used around the room to collect the notes. When each member sticks their note to the flipchart, they should try to stick it next to one on a similar theme already on the flipchart. With the help of the facilitator the team collectively identifies emerging themes and writes headings on the flipcharts.

Clustering: After reading through the notes on each of the flipcharts, team members are encouraged to move the sticky notes to cluster the issues into their appropriate themes.

Prioritise themes: Each person is given a number of different coloured dots. Each dot represents a number of points, for example, black = 1 point, red = 3 points. Each member is given the same amount of dots. Everyone is invited to vote by sticking their dots on which theme they think is most important. The facilitator adds up the points to prioritise which themes are most significant to the team.

The way forward
Using the themes identified the facilitator encourages the team to:

- analyse the root causes;
- develop options to ensure that any successes are not left to chance;
- develop actions to prevent inefficiencies/wasted time re-occurring;
- develop options to mitigate against this issue in the future;
- develop options to repeat/achieve success;
- identify any transferable skills, successful methods, winning strategies.

The root cause analysis utilises various tools, for example the Five whys, and should be facilitated as part of the LFE session/review, as it is the project team who understand the why better than anyone else.

Figure 30 illustrates the typical process for an LFE session.

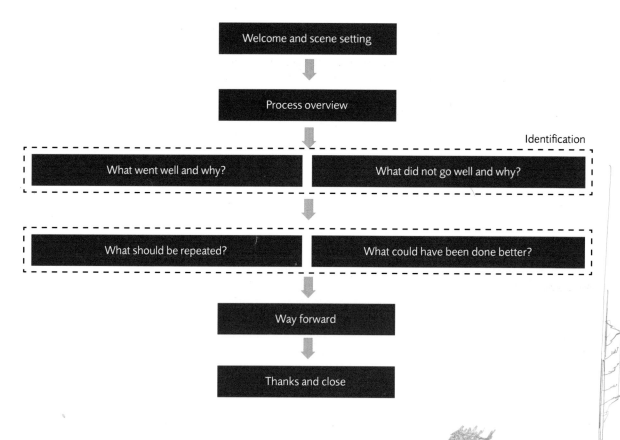

Figure 30 Typical process of a learning from experience session
Reproduced with kind permission from Sellafield Limited

Outputs

- The lessons are documented in a report at the end of each stage and at the end of the overall project, typically by the project manager. The report is stored in a repository or lessons log and is shared with others and is particularly useful in the planning of future projects.
- The report should include the context around the LFE element.
- It is then the responsibility of the lead functions to produce recommendations, engaging subject matter experts as necessary, by comparing with other similar or conflicting lessons learned and by clarifying with the project team as necessary.
- The lessons learned should be communicated to the functional leader and project management community, advising of the new learning point. If relevant, an action plan may be required to resolve the lessons learned.
- The action plan should recommend how the LFE is to be implemented in the existing project controls documentation, which could include project estimates, the WBS construction, checklists, WBS descriptions, task and activity logic, review types and periodicity.
- As soon as the corrective action has been completed, it should be signed off by either the project manager, the knowledge manager or functional leader and this document retained for audit purposes.
- The functional leads are responsible for verifying that appropriate personnel are aware of the learning points in the repository and that any recommendations are being implemented and any actions are closed out.

10.6 The range and scope of learning from experience information requirements

The information available for LFE will be myriad. This section focuses on the information relevant to the application of earned value analysis (EVA).The availability and scope of such information will be influenced by underlying project requirements, processes and tools as well as the ability of the stakeholder community to participate in reviews. The list below is not exhaustive, it represents the typical factors to consider when sourcing information as well as representative data to include:

- key project scope and statistics:
  - scope description;
  - key deliverables and acceptance criteria;
  - project classification.
- size (cost/value, physical and other dimensions);
- sector;
- complexity:
  - time (i.e. start and end dates of each stage) – relevant to, for example, inflation and funding considerations.
- definition:
  - WBS, OBS, RAM, RBS and CBS;
- planning data:
  - as-built programme;
  - methodology and reasons for using;
  - output rates.
- financial data:
  - unit rates and resolution – as applied vs. as available;
  - quantum of change;
  - cash flow;
  - funding.
- data collection:
  - processes including validation process and responsibilities.
- analysis, review and action:
  - performance indicators and variances;
  - EAC;
  - performance reports;
  - data/performance report review feedback (formal and informal).
- change management: for example, what baseline changes were effected, why and how?
- risk management:
  - realised and unrealised risks;
  - mitigated risks;
  - budget vs. cost;
  - management effectiveness.
- communication channels;
- results of formal system reviews (refer to the Systems review section on page 127);
- other:
  - issues – what went well, what didn't?
  - which aspects of EVA were modified during the project and why? For example, the reporting resolution and validation process.

10.7 Issues in the management of the handover of project deliverables

For many projects, the handover of the deliverables is the ultimate culmination of all the project activity. It is therefore important that the handover process is well planned in advance.

The handover process may be very different for different types of project. In particular the project manager should ensure:

* all the project deliverables have been clearly defined and agreed;
* the handover process has been clearly defined and agreed, including the process for dealing with non-conformances or outstanding issues;
* the handover process conforms to organisation guidelines and all relevant checklists have been used;
* all the significant stakeholders are appropriately represented at the handover event.

It is important to consider that poor handover can result in:

* payment delays;
* increased client retentions;
* increased overhead costs (extended insurance, financing, etc.);
* extended resource needs;
* extended warranty requirements;
* delays in equipment availability;
* delays in service to the final client;
* inefficient resource utilisation as work-around solutions are found;
* damage to the client/customer relationship;
* potential penalty costs;
* reduced chance of future work.

10.8 Key stakeholders to be involved in the post-project appraisal

A beneficial review of the data will be achieved by involving the individuals and organisations that have been involved in and/or influenced the project throughout its lifecycle.

When considering who should participate in the post-project appraisal, the stakeholder section of the project management plan should be reviewed, with the following questions asked of each stakeholder:

* were they critical to the delivery of the project or a particular CA?
* were they responsible for delivery of a critical CA?
* how long were they involved with the project?
* are they internal or external to the project organisation?

The key stakeholders identified should be representative of the project context and able to objectively review the EV data and therefore the project performance.

Detailed below is a suggested generic list of key stakeholders that could be involved in the post-project appraisal of EVA:

- project sponsor;
- project manager;
- CAMs;
- project controls managers;
- subject matter experts;
- client representatives;
- key supply chain representatives;
- external stakeholders, for example, local authority, members of the public;
- people involved in related projects who could contribute to or benefit from the review.

10.9 Defining effective learning from experience metrics

Effective performance metrics will depend on the type of project and may be very different for different types of tasks across the breadth of a project. In order to compare performance between projects, it is important that an organisation has a defined set of measures for each type of process.

Project management metrics should include data by reporting period and cumulative figures for contract variance (CV), schedule variance (SV), cost performance index (CPI) and schedule performance index (SPI). This data should be available for every level of the WBS down to the level at which the data was collected. In order to make sense of this data for the LFE, the commentary, issues identified and any variance reports should also be available on a period by period basis.

At a process level, the LFE metrics will depend on the most important performance drivers for the individual process. The process characteristics should also be captured so that similarity with other processes on other projects can be evaluated.

A typical LFE metric could be:

- entries in the LFE register;
- the rate of change in peer to peer observations;
- the frequency of process redesigns;
- the number of close out reviews held.

10.10 Analysing project performance and modifying metrics where appropriate

The analysis of project performance is covered in the Analysis, review and action section starting on page 80, with the selection of appropriate metrics for LFE covered in section 10.9 above.

Project management metrics should be consistent from project to project, while process management metrics should change as:

- processes are redesigned;
- materials change;
- technologies evolve.

These changes should be agreed by the organisation, as new metrics mean that performance can no longer be compared with historic projects. The organisation should resist the temptation to continuously add new metrics without deleting the old ones.

10.11 Reviewing, classifying and prioritising learning from experience

Classifying and prioritising learning should include:

Impact
- Is the impact long term or short term?
- Is the impact safety critical?

Value
- How much time is the learning going to save?
- How much cost is the learning going to save?
- How much is the performance of the product going to improve?

Ease of use
- How easy is it to apply the learning?

Applicability
- How widely applicable is this learning?

Cost effectiveness
- Is the value of this learning worth more than the cost of implementing it?

The resulting evaluation will lead to different communication strategies for the learning.

10.12 Interpreting learning from experience information and making effective recommendations

The interpretation of LFE information and subsequent recommendations could include the points below.

Interpretation
- What was the learning?
- How can that learning be most effectively used to improve organisational and individual performance in the future?

Recommendations
- Changing the process;
- Changing the organisational procedure;
- Changing the people;
- Changing the sub-contractor/supplier;
- Additional training;
- Celebrating and rewarding success;
- Identifying people with different types of experience for use on other tasks and projects;
- Identifying mechanisms, urgency, and breadth of communications required;
- Identifying new metrics and the disposal of old metrics.

10.13 Planning the communication of learning from experience data

The communications plan for the lessons learnt from a project should include:

- the lesson;
- who to share it with;
- what to share;
- when to share;
- how to communicate the lesson.

The integration of knowledge is hard to define explicitly and is best shared by the transfer of experienced personnel from one project to the next or one task to the next.

Component design knowledge or experience is easier to define explicitly and is most easily shared using a lessons learnt database that other personnel can search.

10.14 Selecting and matching the experience of individuals with project requirements

Certain types of LFE are best utilised by transferring personnel from one project to the next, or one task to the next. In order to use this experience, an organisation needs to know what type of experience is required on a new project task, and who in the organisation has that experience.

Tasks on a project that benefit from experienced personnel need to be highlighted for special consideration. The organisation needs to maintain a database of individuals, the roles they have undertaken on projects and the experience they have gained.

When a new team is being recruited for a new task or project, this database needs to be consulted to ensure that those with the appropriate recent experience are effectively used on the most beneficial tasks on the next project.

10.15 Defining the project closedown process

The project closedown process should include:

- the demobilisation of the project team;
- the identification of lessons learnt;
- the handover to a support organisation (if required);
- the closedown of the project on the accounting and management systems;
- the acceptance of the work by the customer.

These processes should be defined in the organisation's procedures. Planning the closedown involves tailoring these procedures for specific projects. Provisional planning for closedown should be done early in the project lifecycle.

10.16 The effectiveness of the learning from experience regime for a specific project and organisation

It is important to consider whether the LFE regime complies with the guidelines detailed in the rest of this section. In particular:

Does it have different ways of sharing LFE:
- by type of knowledge?
- by urgency of need?

how good is it at:
- capturing learning (people and knowledge)?
- evaluating learning?
- communicating learning?
- using the learning?

does it take opportunities to share learning:
- within teams?
- within projects?
- with other projects?
- within the supply chain?

11 The Earned Value 32 Criteria

The criteria have been reproduced with minor amendments from the industry standard (American National Standards Institute, 1998) and are organised in five major categories.

A.1 ORGANISATION

1. Define the authorised work elements for the project. A work breakdown structure (WBS), tailored for effective internal management control, is commonly used in this process.
   Paraphrase of criterion: Define authorised work and resources via contract work breakdown structure (CWBS).
2. Identify the project organisational structure, including the major sub-contractors responsible for achieving the authorised work, and define the organisational elements in which work will be planned and controlled.
   Paraphrase of criterion: Establish organisational responsibility for work achievement via OBS.
3. Provide for the integration of the project's planning, scheduling, budgeting, work authorisation and cost accumulation processes with each other and, as appropriate, the work breakdown structure and the organisational structure.
   Paraphrase of criterion: Ensure management subsystems support each other, the CWBS and the OBS.
4. Identify the organisation responsible for controlling overhead (indirect costs).
   Paraphrase of criterion: Identify who is responsible for overhead cost control.
5. Provide for integration of the project work breakdown structure and the project organisational structure in a manner that permits cost and schedule performance measurement by elements of either or both structures as needed.
   Paraphrase of criterion: Integrate CWBS with OBS.

A.2 PLANNING, SCHEDULING AND BUDGETING

6. Schedule the authorised work in a manner that describes the sequence of work and identifies significant task interdependencies required to meet the requirements of the project.
   Paraphrase of criterion: Schedule all authorised work logically.
7. Identify physical products, milestones, technical performance goals or other indicators that will be used to measure progress.
   Paraphrase of criterion: Identify interim goals (milestones) by which to measure work achievement.
8. Establish and maintain a time-phased budget baseline, at the control account level, against which project performance can be measured. Budget for far-term efforts may be held in higher-level accounts until an appropriate time for allocation at the control account level. Initial budgets established for performance measurement will be based on either internal management goals or the external customer negotiated target cost including estimates for authorised but undefinitised work. If an over-target baseline (OTB) is used for performance measurement reporting purposes, prior notification must be provided to the appropriate senior manager and customer (if required).
   Paraphrase of criterion: Establish/maintain at the control account level a performance measurement baseline.
9. Establish budgets for authorised work, with identification of significant cost elements (labour, material etc.) as needed for internal management and for control of sub-contractors.
   Paraphrase of criterion: Establish budgets by element of cost.
10. To the extent it is practical to identify the authorised work in discrete work packages, establish budgets for this work in terms of money, hours, or other measurable units. Where the entire control account is not subdivided into work packages, identify the far-term effort in larger planning packages for budget and scheduling purposes.
    Paraphrase of criterion: Establish budgets at the work/planning package level.
11. Provide that the sum of all work package budgets plus planning package budgets within a control account equals the control account budget.
    Paraphrase of criterion: Sum of all WP = PP budget = Budget CA.
12. Identify and control level of effort activity by time-phased budgets established for this purpose. Only that effort which is unmeasurable or for which measurement is impractical may be classified as level of effort.

Paraphrase of criterion: Separately identify and control the use of LoE.

13. Establish overhead budgets for each significant organisational component of the company for expenses which will become indirect costs. Reflect in the project budgets, at the appropriate level, the amounts in overhead pools that are planned to be allocated to the project as indirect costs.
Paraphrase of criterion: Establish budgets for overhead costs.

14. Identify management reserves and undistributed budget.
Paraphrase of criterion: Identify MR and UB separately.

15. Provide that the project target cost goal is reconciled with the sum of all internal project budgets and management reserves.
Paraphrase of criterion: CBB = BAC = MR.

A.3 ACCOUNTING CONSIDERATIONS

16. Record direct costs in a manner consistent with the budgets in a formal system controlled by the general books of account.
Paraphrase of criterion: Formally record all direct costs and establish budgets in a consistent and thus comparable manner.

17. Summarise direct costs from control accounts into the work breakdown structure without allocation of a single control account to two or more work breakdown structure elements.
Paraphrase of criterion: Prohibit multiple accounting as direct costs are summarised through the WBS.

18. Summarise direct costs from the control accounts into the organisational structure without allocation of a single control account to two or more organisational elements.
Paraphrase of criterion: Prohibit multiple accounting as direct costs are summarised through the OBS.

19. Record all indirect costs that will be allocated to the contract.
Paraphrase of criterion: Record all allocable indirect costs.

20. Identify unit costs, equivalent unit costs or lot costs when needed.
Paraphrase of criterion: Identify applicable unit costs.

21. For EVMS, the material accounting system will provide for:
    (1) accurate cost accumulation and assignment of costs to control accounts in a manner consistent with the budgets using recognised, acceptable, costing techniques;
    (2) cost performance measurement at the point in time most suitable for the category of material involved, but no earlier than the time of progress payments or actual receipt of material;
    (3) full accountability of all material purchased for the project including the residual inventory.
    Paraphrase of criterion: Establish an acceptable material accounting system.

A.4 ANALYSIS AND MANAGEMENT REPORTS

22. At least on a monthly basis, generate the following information at the control account and other levels as necessary for management control using actual cost data from, or reconcilable with, the accounting system:
    1. comparison of the amount of planned budget and the amount of budget earned for work achieved – this comparison provides the schedule variance;
    2. comparison of the amount of the budget earned and the actual (applied/estimated where appropriate) direct costs for the same work – this comparison provides the cost variance.
    Paraphrase of criterion: Identify performance measurement data elements at the CA level on a monthly basis.

23. Identify, at least monthly, the significant differences between both planned and actual schedule performance and planned and actual cost performance, and provide the reasons for the variances in the detail needed by project management.
Paraphrase of criterion: Identify schedule and cost deviations on at least a monthly basis.

24. Identify budgeted and applied (or actual) indirect costs at the level and frequency needed by management for effective control, along with the reasons for any significant variances.
Paraphrase of criterion: Identify overhead performance measurement data as needed.

25. Summarise the data elements and associated variances through the project organisation and/or work breakdown structure to support management needs and any customer reporting specified in the contract.
Paraphrase of criterion: Sum up performance measurement data elements through the CWBS and OBS.
26. Implement managerial actions taken as the result of earned value information.
Paraphrase of criterion: Identify management response to variances.
27. Develop revised estimates of cost at completion based on performance to date, commitment values for material and estimates of future conditions. Compare this information with the performance measurement baseline to identify variances at completion important to company management and any applicable customer reporting requirements.
Paraphrase of criterion: Develop EACs and compare with staffing plans and the CBB.

A.5   REVISIONS AND DATA MAINTENANCE

28. Incorporate authorised changes in a timely manner, recording the effects of such changes in budgets and schedules. In the directed effort prior to negotiation of a change, base such revisions on the amount estimated and budgeted to the project organisations.
Paraphrase of criterion: Incorporate all authorised changes in a timely manner.
29. Reconcile current budgets to prior budgets in terms of changes to the authorised work and internal re-planning in the detail needed by management for effective control.
Paraphrase of criterion: Reconcile original budgets with current budgets.
30. Control retroactive changes to records pertaining to work performed that would change previously reported amounts for actual costs, earned value or budgets. Adjustments should be made only for correction of errors, routine accounting adjustments, effects of customer or management directed changes, or to improve the baseline integrity and accuracy of performance measurement data.
Paraphrase of criterion: Control retroactive changes to records.
31. Prevent revisions to the project budget except for authorised changes.
Paraphrase of criterion: Only the senior manager or the customer may revise the CBB.
32. Document changes to the performance measurement baseline.
Paraphrase of criterion: Document PMB changes.

12 Earned Value equations

Basic formulae

1. Cost variance

CV = BCWP – ACWP

Positive/negative indicates under/over planned cost for work performed.

2. Cost variance percentage

$$CV\% = \frac{CV}{BCWP} \times 100$$

3. Cost performance index

$$CPI = \frac{BCWP}{ACWP}$$

Indicates whether work accomplished so far has been completed within budget. Over/under 1.0 indicates greater/lesser efficiency.

4. Schedule variance

SV = BCWP – BCWS

Positive/negative indicates ahead/behind planned schedule.

5. Schedule variance percentage

$$SV\% = \frac{SV}{BCWS} \times 100$$

6. Schedule performance index

$$SPI = \frac{BCWP}{BCWS}$$

Indicates whether work accomplished so far has been achieved to schedule.
Over/under 1.0 indicates greater/lesser than schedule achievement.

7. Schedule variance in months

$$SV\ (months) = \frac{SV\ (cum)}{Average\ Monthly\ BCWP}$$

Independent statistical forecast formulae

1. Estimate at completion

IEAC = ACWP + ETC

Extrapolations of future cost assuming past performance include:

2. Independent estimate to completion

$$\text{IETC} = \frac{(BAC-BCWP)}{CP}$$

3. Independent estimate at completion

$$\text{IETC} = ACWP + \frac{(BAC-BCWP)}{(CP \times SP)}$$

4. To complete performance index for planned budget

$$\text{TCPI(BAC)} = \frac{(BAC-BCWP)}{(BAC-ACWP)}$$

5. To complete performance index for estimated out-turn costs

$$\text{TCPI(EAC)} = \frac{(BAC-BCWP)}{(EAC-ACWP)}$$

To calculate the future cost performance index required to meet the estimated out-turn costs

Other formulae

1. Percentage spent

$$\%\text{spent} = \frac{ACWP}{BAC} \times 100$$

2. Percentage complete

$$\%\text{compt} = \frac{BCWP}{BAC} \times 100$$

3. Variance at completion

VAC = BAC – EAC

4. Variance at completion percentage

$$\text{VAC\%} = \frac{VAC}{BAC} \times 100$$

13 References and further reading

Association of Project Management (2010) *Introduction to Project Control*, APM: Princes Risborough.
ISBN: 978-1-903494-34-9

Association of Project Management (2010) *The Earned Value Management Compass*, APM: Princes Risborough.
ISBN: 978-1-903494-33-2

Association of Project Management (2008) *Introduction to Project Planning*, APM: Princes Risborough.
ISBN: 978-1-903494-28-8

Association of Project Management (2008) *Earned Value Management: APM Guidelines*, APM: Princes Risborough.
ISBN: 978-1-903494-26-4

Association of Project Management (2008) *Interfacing Risk and Earned Value Management*, APM: Princes Risborough.
ISBN: 978-1-903494-24-0

Association of Project Management (2006) *APM Body of Knowledge (5th edition)*, APM: Princes Risborough.
ISBN: 1-903494-13-3

All the above titles are available from www.apm.org.uk

A Guide to Conducting Integrated Baseline Reviews, Issue No 3, (DEVMIG), July 2009

14 List of figures

List of tables

Earned value abbreviations and acronyms

ACWP	Actual Cost of Work Performed
AE	Apportioned Effort
AF	Apportioned Factor
ATE	Actual Time Expended
AUW	Authorised Un-priced Work
BAC	Budget At Completion
BCWP	Budgeted Cost of Work Performed
BCWR	Budgeted Cost of Work Remaining
BCWS	Budgeted Cost of Work Scheduled
BoE	Basis of Estimate
BSI	British Standards Institute
CA	Control Account
CAM	Control Account Manager
CAP	Cost Account Plan
CBB	Contract Budget Baseline
CPI	Cost Performance Index
CPM	Critical Path Method
CPR	Cost Performance Report
CTC	Contract Target Cost
CV	Cost Variance
CV%	Cost variance percentage
CWBS	Contract Work Breakdown Structure
DB	Distributed Budget
EAC	Estimate At Completion
EMV	Expected Monetary Value
ETC	Estimate To Completion
EV	Earned Value
EVA	Earned Value Analysis
EVM	Earned Value Management
EVMS	Earned Value Management System
EVT	Earned Value Technique
IBR	Integrated Baseline Review
IMS	Integrated Master Schedule
ISO	International Standards Organisation
LoE	Level of Effort
LRE	Latest Revised Estimate (same as EAC)
MR	Management Reserve
OBS	Organisation Breakdown Structure
OD	Original Duration
ODC	Other Direct Costs
OTB	Over-Target Baseline
PF	Performance Factor
PCS	Project Control System
PMB	Performance Measurement Baseline

PMS	Project Master Schedule
PP	Planning Package
PV	Planned Value
RAM	Responsibility Assignment Matrix
RMA	Risk Mitigation Action
RM	Risk Management
SoR	Statement of Requirement
SoW	Statement of Work
SPI	Schedule Performance Index
SV	Schedule Variance
SV%	Schedule Variance percentage
TAB	Total Allocated Budget
TCPI	To Complete Performance Index
UB	Undistributed Budget
VAC	Variance At Completion
VAC%	Variance At Completion percentage
VAR	Variance Analysis Report
WBS	Work Breakdown Structure
WBSD	Work Breakdown Structure Dictionary
WP	Work Package

Glossary

Activity. An element of work performed during the course of a project. An activity normally has an expected duration, an expected cost, and expected resource requirements. Activities are often subdivided into tasks.

Acceptance criteria. A prioritised set of criteria that the project product must meet before the customer will accept it, i.e. measurable definitions of the attributes required for the set of products to be acceptable to key stakeholders.

Baseline. See Performance Measurement Baseline.

Benefit. The measurable improvement resulting from an outcome perceived as an advantage by one or more stakeholders.

Budget. The resources (in money and/or hours) assigned for the accomplishment of a specific task or group of tasks.

Buffer. A term used in critical chain. Also used in the risk management sense for contingency allocated to a schedule after confidence modelling has been conducted.

Business As Usual (BAU). One or more repeatable activities that relate to the day-to-day operation of a company or organisation.

Change control. A process that ensures that all changes made to a project's baseline scope, time, cost or quality objectives are identified, evaluated, approved, rejected or deferred.

Critical path. A sequence of activities through a project network or schedule from start to finish, the sum of whose durations determines the overall project duration. There may be more than one such path. The path through a series of activities, taking into account interdependencies, in which the late completion activities will have an impact on the project end date or delay a key milestone.

Customer*. The person or group who commissioned the work and will benefit from the end results.

Deliverable (or output). A specialist product that is handed over to the user(s).

Deterministic. Something with an outcome that is already known, with no possibility of that outcome changing.

Earliest start date. The earliest possible date when an activity can start within the logical and imposed constraints of the network.

Earned Value. The value of completed work expressed in terms of the budget assigned to that work.

Earned Value Management (EVM). A best practice project control process that is based on a structured approach to planning, cost collection and performance measurement. It facilitates the integration of project scope, schedule, cost, risk and resource objectives and the establishment of a baseline plan for performance measurement.

Emergent risks. Those risks that have been identified through early warning indicators and trend analysis but require more development before being approved by the Project Board.

Enterprise. The aggregation of project, programme, Business As Usual and Portfolio activities within an organisation that make up its business.

Estimate. An approximation of project time and cost targets, refined throughout the project lifecycle.

Free float. The time by which an activity may be either delayed or extended without affecting the start of any succeeding activity.

Independent authority. An individual, team, or organisation that has no link to the project, programme or BAU undergoing the maturity process and is not unduly or unfairly influenced by those within the organisation's management structure. Such an authority can be internal or external to the organisation, depending on the nature and context of the assessment.

Integrated Master Schedule (IMS). A schedule that is generated from other schedules, usually from different parts of the project contract supply chain. The result of the vertical and/or horizontal linking of these through key activities or milestones.

Key deliverables. Those items that are linked to the satisfaction of key requirements. If delivery of these key items is not met within time, cost or quality limits, then this will directly affect the delivery of the entire project or programme.

Latest finish date. The latest possible date by which an activity has to finish within the logical activity and imposed constraints of the network, without affecting the total project duration.

Lag. In a network diagram, the minimum necessary lapse of time between the finish of one activity and the finish of an overlapping activity. The delay incurred between two specified activities.

Lessons learned. The identification of activities associated with the project that went well, and those that could have been better, to recommend improvements applied in the future and to future projects.

Management Information System (MIS). A collection of tools and applications that are used to manipulate data from management products to enable decisions to be made about a specific project(s) or programme(s).

Management Reserve (MR). An amount of the total allocated budget withheld for management control purposes rather than designated for the achievement of a specific task or set of tasks. It is not a part of the Performance Measurement Baseline.

Milestone. An activity of zero duration principally used to enhance the clarity of the programme structure.

Mitigation Action (risk response). Actions that may be taken to bring a situation to a level where exposure to risk is acceptable to the organisation. These responses fall into a number of risk response categories.

Negative lag. See Lag.

Network diagram. Any schematic display of the logical relationships of project activities. Always drawn from left to right to reflect project chronology.

Non Specific Risk Provision (NSRP). The amount of budget/schedule/resources set aside to cover the impact of emergent risks, should they occur.

Organisation Breakdown Structure (OBS). A functionally oriented code established to identity the performance responsibility for work on a specific contract.

Partner. An organisation or business that has entered into a legally binding agreement with another party to manage a contract between them. Distinct from a legal partnership.

Performance Measurement Baseline (PMB). The time-phased budget plan against which contract performance is measured. It is formed by the budgets assigned to scheduled control accounts and the applicable indirect budgets. For future effort, not planned to the control account level, the performance measurement baseline also includes budgets assigned to higher level WBS elements and undistributed budgets. It equals the total allocated budget less management reserve.

Planning. The process of identifying the means, resources and actions necessary to accomplish an objective.

Project Management Office (PMO). An organisation that is responsible for the governance infrastructure of P3 management.

Positive lag. See Lag.

Programme controls. The application of processes to measure programme performance against the programme plan, to enable variances to be identified and corrected, so that programme objectives are achieved.

Project controls. The application of processes to measure project performance against the project plan, to enable variances to be identified and corrected, so that project objectives are achieved.

Recurring elements. Those schedule elements that are by their nature not unique and are repeated more than once throughout the project or programme phases – for example, production, logistic support or BAU activities (security checks, governance reviews etc.)

Red/Amber/Green (RAG). A term used to indicate the status of a variable when compared with a set of predefined levels or criteria.

Responsibility Assignment Matrix (RAM). A depiction of the relationship between the Contract Work Breakdown Structure elements and the organisations assigned responsibility for ensuring their accomplishment.

Schedule. A schedule is the timetable for a project. It shows how project activities and milestones are planned over a period of time. It is often shown as either a milestone chart, Gantt chart or other bar chart, or a tabulated series of dates.

Scheduling. The process used to determine the overall project duration. This includes identification of activities and their logical dependencies, and estimating activity durations, taking into account requirements and availability of resources. Not to be confused with planning.

Schedule Risk Analysis (SRA). A technique used to understand the effect of project risks on the early and late start and finish dates of activities and milestones within the schedule. It is used as part of the buffer allocation process.

Schedule Variance (SV). A metric for the schedule performance on a programme. It is the difference between earned value and the budget (Schedule Variance = Earned Value - Budget). A positive value is a favourable condition while a negative value is unfavourable.

Significant Variances. Those differences between planned and actual performance, which require further review, analysis, or action. Appropriate thresholds should be established as to the magnitude of variances that will automatically require variance analysis.

Stakeholder. Any individual, group or organisation that can affect, be affected by, or perceive itself to be affected by, an initiative (programme, project, activity, risk.)

Steering board. A group, usually comprising the sponsor, senior managers and sometimes key stakeholders, whose remit is to set the strategic direction of the project. It gives guidance to the project manager. Often referred to as the steering group or project board.

Supplier*. The person, group or groups responsible for the supply of the project's specialist products.

Total float. The time by which an activity may be either delayed or extended without either affecting the total project duration or violating a target finish date.

Threshold. Acceptable cost and schedule variations from the baseline. Typically, thresholds are based on either a value or a percentage of the budget.

Uncertainty. A state of incomplete knowledge about a proposition. Usually associated with risks, both threats and opportunities.

Variances. See Significant Variances.

Work Breakdown Structure (WBS). A product-oriented family tree division of hardware, software, services and other work tasks which organises, defines, and graphically displays the product to be produced as well as the work to be achieved to achieve the specified product.

* Asterisks indicate definitions that are also published in BS6079-2:2000. Permission to reproduce extracts of BS6079:2000 is granted by BSI. British Standards can be obtained from BSI customer services, 389 Chiswick High Road, London, W4 4AL, tel: +44(0)20 89969001. Email cservices@bsi-global.com

Section index